PRAISE FOR **PLANET**

"With *Planet Narnia*, Michael Ward has established himself not only as the foremost living Lewis scholar, but also as a brilliant writer. . . . His cumulative case for reading the Narnia books in terms of the planets is overwhelming. . . . This introduction to a masterpiece is something of a masterpiece in its own right."

Times Literary Supplement

"[*Planet Narnia*] is, to all appearances, a gamble of presumptuous proportions; but it pays off powerfully and persuasively . . . [Ward] makes a marvellous case . . . profound . . . striking . . . brilliant."

The Independent on Sunday

"An argument which is at once subtle and sensible, a combination not often found in modern academic writing. . . . This is an outstanding guide not only to Narnia, but also to Lewis's thinking as a whole, and to the 'genial' medieval world-view which he so much loved."

Books & Culture

"I cannot contain my admiration. No other book on Lewis has ever shown such comprehensive knowledge of his works and such depth of insight. This will make Michael Ward's name."

Walter Hooper, Literary adviser to the Estate of C. S. Lewis and author of C. S. Lewis, A Companion and Guide

"Noting Michael Ward's claim that he has discovered 'the secret imaginative key' to the Narnia books, the sensible reader responds by erecting a castle of skepticism. My own castle was gradually but utterly demolished as I read this thoughtful, scholarly, and vividly-written book."

Alan Jacobs, Professor of English at Wheaton College and author of The Narnian: The Life and Imagination of C. S. Lewis

"Michael Ward's *Planet Narnia* is an example of a very rare species: a work of literary detection which, despite the breathtaking daring of its central thesis, is utterly convincing and compelling. . . . The pieces fall into place with the combined thrill of an aesthetic, intellectual and spiritual satisfaction. . . . Reading the Narnia books will, in the best sense, never be the same again—not that anything will be lost, but that an entire new layer of understanding will be present."

N. T. Wright, Professor of New Testament and Early Christianity at the University of St. Andrews and author of Surprised by Hope

"Michael Ward presents an absorbing, learned analysis of C. S. Lewis's bestselling and beloved series, the Chronicles of Narnia. Readily accessible to the average reader, Ward's book reads so much like a detective story that it's difficult to put down."

Armand M. Nicholi, Jr., Professor of Psychiatry at Harvard Medical School and author of The Question of God: C. S. Lewis and Sigmund Freud

"This feat of scholarly detective work will absorb your attention from start to finish. Michael Ward proposes a heretofore unnoticed structure that unifies the Chronicles of Narnia, based on Lewis's lifelong engagement with medieval astrology. . . . The result is both surprising and persuasive."

Christianity Today

"Brilliantly conceived. Intellectually provocative. Rhetorically convincing. A panegyric is not the usual way to begin a book review, but Michael Ward's *Planet Narnia: The Seven Heavens in the Imagination of C. S. Lewis* is worthy of such praise. I do not mean to suggest it is a perfect book, yet what Ward attempts—the first rigorously comprehensive reading of C. S. Lewis's Chronicles of Narnia—is magisterial . . . stimulating and engaging . . . important . . . thoughtful, informed, perceptive. . . . Every serious student of Lewis should buy *Planet Narnia*. In effect, it is the starting point from now forward for all serious scholarly discussions of the Chronicles of Narnia."

Christianity and Literature

"An exciting synthesis of mystery story and literary scholarship . . . Ward is a master code-breaker. . . . He reveals previously overlooked connections by means of both broad brush-strokes and intricate details. . . . This procedure results in a grand literary adventure through the cosmos and through a great writer's mind. . . . If more scholars wrote such enchanting prose and discovered such compelling secrets, we would take volumes of literary criticism to the beach for summer reading."

Sehnsucht: The C. S. Lewis Journal

THE NARNIA CODE

C. S. LEWIS
AND THE SECRET
OF THE
SEVEN HEAVENS

MICHAEL WARD

Tyndale House Publishers, Inc.
Carol Stream, Illinois

Library of Congress Cataloging-in-Publication Data

Ward, Michael, date.
    The Narnia code : C.S. Lewis and the secret of the seven heavens / Michael Ward.
        p. cm.
    Rev. ed. of: Planet Narnia.
    Includes bibliographical references and index.
    ISBN 978-1-4143-3965-8 (sc)
    1. Lewis, C. S. (Clive Staples), 1898-1963. Chronicles of Narnia. 2. Lewis, C. S. (Clive Staples), 1898-1963—Religion. 3. Lewis, C. S. (Clive Staples), 1898-1963—Knowledge and learning. I. Lewis, C. S. (Clive Staples), 1898-1963. Planet Narnia. II. Title.
PR6023.E926Z944 2010
823'.912—dc22   2010029274

Printed in the United States of America

16   15   14   13   12   11   10
 7   6   5   4   3   2   1

To

Tyler Blanski

who loves the Morning Star

and to ~~Angela~~ Dethlon
with Jovial regards
from Michael Ward

The heavens are telling the glory of God;
*   and the firmament proclaims his handiwork.*
Day to day pours forth speech,
*   and night to night declares knowledge.*
There is no speech, nor are there words;
*   their voice is not heard;*
yet their voice goes out through all the earth,
*   and their words to the end of the world.*

PSALM 19:1-4

"The greatest poem in the Psalter and one of the greatest lyrics in the world."
C. S. Lewis, writing about Psalm 19 in *Reflections on the Psalms*

CONTENTS

A NOTE ABOUT THE AUTHOR

MICHAEL WARD was born in Cuckfield, Sussex, England. He is an ordained minister in the Anglican Church and works as chaplain of St. Peter's College, Oxford, and as a tutor and lecturer. He has loved the Narnia Chronicles since he was a boy.

He first wrote about C. S. Lewis while working for his English degree at the University of Oxford. He lived at Lewis's former home in Oxford, The Kilns, as resident warden for three years (1996–1999), sleeping in the late professor's old bedroom and studying in his study. He appeared in *Shadowlands*, the film about Lewis's marriage and bereavement. He also helped run the Oxford Lewis Society for many years before moving to Cambridge to study theology. He did his PhD at the University of St. Andrews, and his dissertation was published as *Planet Narnia: The Seven Heavens in the Imagination of C. S. Lewis* (Oxford University Press, 2008). The British Broadcasting Corporation (BBC) commissioned and broadcast a television documentary about *Planet Narnia* called *The Narnia Code* in 2009. The success of *Planet Narnia* and the TV documentary led to the book you now hold in your hands.

Dr. Ward has written numerous scholarly articles on C. S. Lewis and has lectured all around the world on his life and work. He is also the coeditor of *The Cambridge Companion to C. S. Lewis* (2010) and *Heresies and How to Avoid Them: Why It Matters What Christians Believe* (2007).

Aside from his work as a college chaplain and Lewis scholar, Michael serves as associate editor of Davey's Daily Poetry, the online poetry service.

For more information about the author, see **www.michaelward.net**.

A Note about the Order of the Chronicles

The order in which Lewis published the Narnia Chronicles is:

The Lion, the Witch and the Wardrobe (1950)
Prince Caspian (1951)
The Voyage of the "Dawn Treader" (1952)
The Silver Chair (1953)
The Horse and His Boy (1954)
The Magician's Nephew (1955)
The Last Battle (1956)

Most Lewis scholars agree that *The Lion, the Witch and the Wardrobe* should be read first because it was written first and published first and takes special care to introduce the character of Aslan. *The Magician's Nephew* should therefore not be read first, even though it deals with an earlier stage in Narnian history. It is better to read it as a flashback or a prequel.

CHAPTER ONE

THE MYSTERY

For those outside everything is in parables;
so that they may indeed see but not perceive,
and may indeed hear but not understand.

MARK 4:11-12

Do you remember when you first heard the story of Lucy Pevensie pushing her way through the back of a wardrobe and finding herself in a snowy wood? Do you recall how you felt when Lucy had tea with Mr. Tumnus and learned that his world, the kingdom of Narnia, was ruled by an evil White Witch, who had banished the old days of jollification? Undoubtedly, *The Lion, the Witch and the Wardrobe* contains one of literature's greatest fairy-tale openings.

I first followed Lucy as she entered the wardrobe when I was a young boy—too young to read for myself, but not too young to be read to. My older brothers and I jumped into our parents' bed one Sunday morning, and my mother read aloud the opening chapter from *The Lion, the*

Witch and the Wardrobe. We loved it. Sunday by Sunday, the Ward family worked its way through the whole book, and eventually through the six other Narnia Chronicles as well.

GIVE FATHER CHRISTMAS THE SACK!

But one thing surprised me about *The Lion, the Witch and the Wardrobe,* and that was when Father Christmas appeared. I didn't expect to meet Santa in Narnia. I was glad he was there, of course, and I was pleased when he gave out the presents. But I somehow felt that Father Christmas belonged to a different kind of story world.

When I got older and began to study Lewis's works more seriously, I discovered that many other people felt the same way. In fact, one of these people, Roger Lancelyn Green, a good friend of Lewis's, had urged him to leave out Father Christmas.

Why had Lewis kept him in? It didn't make sense. Father Christmas is a character who represents the festival of Christ's birth, yet no one in Narnia ever shows any knowledge of a character called Christ. They know only of the Christlike lion Aslan. How, then, do the Narnians know of Christmas? What do they *mean* by Christmas? It looks like an elementary mistake on Lewis's part.

Several other scholars have made the same complaint as Roger Lancelyn Green. They say the appearance of Father Christmas "strikes the wrong note";* it's "incongruous." One expert said that "to be true to his fantasy world, Lewis should perhaps have created a Narnian equivalent to our Christmas instead of taking it into Narnia."

Admittedly, a character called Father Aslanmas sounds awkward and wouldn't have been a good idea, but it would have made much better *logical* sense. Better still to have left Father Christmas out entirely—or so I felt.

This puzzle about Father Christmas was the beginning for me of

*References for all quotations may be found in the Notes section starting on page 161.

the great Narnian mystery. *The Lion, the Witch and the Wardrobe* is a powerful and attractive story, and yet it seems, on the face of it, to have a weakness that a six-year-old could identify. How could this be?

Perhaps it was simply a careless error on Lewis's part, indicating that he hadn't given much thought to the story. But that seems unlikely, given that he included Father Christmas even *after* hearing Green's objections. It may have been a mistake, but it wasn't a *careless* error! Lewis clearly thought there was good reason to keep Father Christmas in the story.

But what was that reason? It was a question I wanted the answer to.

I continued to ponder the oddity of Father Christmas's appearance in *The Lion, the Witch and the Wardrobe* even as my family moved on to the next books in the series. And then I noticed mysterious things in the other Chronicles as well:

- The Roman god Bacchus organizes a kind of riot in *Prince Caspian* and makes everyone merry with wine—*but does Bacchus really belong to that story?* I wondered.
- And how come the children fail to recognize Prince Rilian in *The Silver Chair*? It was obvious to me that the young man in black clothes was the lost prince they were looking for, and I couldn't see why it took them so long to realize it.
- Perhaps the greatest mystery of all was *The Horse and His Boy*, which seemed to me just one long journey across a desert.

THE GOOD BOOK AND THE SEVEN GOOD BOOKS

Early on, I was baffled by the series on another level. We were a church-going family, and my parents told me that some of the characters in Narnia were linked to biblical characters. Aslan, the lion king, was rather like Jesus, they said. Just as Aslan died on the Stone Table in order to rescue the guilty Edmund from the hands of the White Witch before returning to life, so Jesus died on the cross to save people from sin and then rose from the grave. Lewis himself (so I later learned) once wrote to a child explaining that the whole Narnia series was "about Christ."

I liked the idea that there was a second level of meaning to *The Lion, the Witch and the Wardrobe*. And I could see biblical connections in some of the other books too. The way Aslan sang Narnia into being in *The Magician's Nephew* was a bit like God creating the world in Genesis. *The Last Battle* was like God's judgment on the world in the book of Revelation.

What was mystifying was that the biblical links in the other four Narnia Chronicles were not half so obvious. In fact, they were barely present by comparison. Yes, Aslan was still there, and he was still like Jesus in various ways (guiding, teaching, forgiving, and so forth), but there was no clear connection between the overall story and any major episode in Jesus' life or ministry.

- In *Prince Caspian* Aslan enters the story among dancing trees before giving a great war cry. *What does that have to do with Jesus?* I wondered.
- In *The Voyage of the "Dawn Treader"* Aslan rips off a dragon skin, is made visible by a magic spell, and flies along a sunbeam like a bird. You could find biblical sources for these things if you tried hard enough, but what tied them together? I was curious.
- In *The Silver Chair* Aslan doesn't appear bodily in Narnia but stays in his own high country above the clouds—as if Jesus had gone back to being just "God in heaven" rather than "God with us."
- And in *The Horse and His Boy* (on top of its long journey across the desert that so perplexed me), Aslan is mistaken for two lions, or maybe three lions, and does a great deal of dashing about. He is said to be "swift of foot." Now, why would you make your Jesus-like character "swift of foot"? Jesus is never shown running in the Bible!

Jesus' birth, of course, *is* recorded in the Bible and is obviously a very important event—on par with Creation, salvation, and the final judgment—yet (as I have already pointed out) there's no Narnian version of Christmas, no story about Aslan being born as a cub in Narnia like Jesus was born as a baby in Bethlehem. Nor is there a Narnian version of the Ascension, when Jesus returned to heaven. Nor is there a Narnian Day of Pentecost, when the Christian church was born.

Since three of the Chronicles were clearly connected to biblical passages in Genesis, the Gospels, and Revelation, I thought it strange that the remaining four Chronicles weren't as clearly linked to other major events in the Bible story.

In short, the Narnia books were as mysterious on their second level (the level of biblical parallels) as they were mysterious on their first level (the level of the basic story).

"EVERY CHAPTER BETTER THAN THE ONE BEFORE"

Although I was occasionally puzzled as a young reader, I still hugely enjoyed the series in general. In fact, I adored it. Reepicheep and Puddleglum were the two standout characters. The Wood between the Worlds in *The Magician's Nephew* fascinated me. I laughed at the foolish monopods in *The Voyage of the "Dawn Treader,"* and I grieved when Father Time brought the whole sequence to a close at the end of *The Last Battle.* I wished I could join the characters in that heavenly story "which goes on forever: in which every chapter is better than the one before."

What a vital, colorful world Narnia was! Perky jackdaws cracking jokes. Guilty dragons made soft and tender. Castles shining like stars on the seashore. Despite being confused at times about his mysterious methods, I thought C. S. Lewis was simply the *best* author. I was a bookish boy, so I had lots of other stories to compare his work with. Without a doubt, the Chronicles were my favorites.

At school, when my teacher asked the class to make a picture representing the storybook we liked most, it was easy to know what to do. I drew three silhouettes: one of a lion, one of a witch, and one of a wardrobe. I then filled them in with different crayons: gold for the lion, white for the witch, brown for the wardrobe. And finally I put them through a typewriter (we still had typewriters in those days, not computers) and typed "cslewiscslewiscslewis" back and forth across each silhouette. I was very proud of the resulting picture, and I remembered it thirty years later when one night, while I was a student at Cambridge University, quite unexpectedly I had the idea that led to this book. We will come back to those silhouettes in the final chapter.

DID HE PLAN IT?

Yet as I eagerly immersed myself in the series on one hand, I continued pondering its mysteries. The question came down to this: Was it possible there was a *third* level of meaning that tied together all the puzzling elements—or were the books planless, without a governing logic?

The answer most people have given is that Lewis was deliberately drawing on a rich and wide range of traditions as he created the world of Narnia. They suggest there was no particular logic to his choices—apart from the very loose and vague logic expressed in the old proverb "Variety is the spice of life." "Don't press too hard," they imply. "These are only children's books! They're not to be taken seriously. Narnia is a glorious hodgepodge, nothing more."

Many reviewers have thought the books are effectively planless—just Lewis having fun and not taking much care how. One critic describes Narnia as a "jumble," "full of inconsistencies." Another critic says the Chronicles are "uneven" and "hastily written." A third critic thinks Lewis wrote "glibly" in a "whizz-bang, easy-come-easy-go, slap-it-down kind of way."

One primary reason critics think this is because Lewis's great friend

J. R. R. Tolkien thought so. Lewis read *The Lion, the Witch and the Wardrobe* aloud to Tolkien, who hated it. Yes, *hated* it! In Tolkien's view, Lewis had thrown together things from different traditions (talking animals, English children, fauns and centaurs, Father Christmas, etc.) without good cause.

Tolkien so detested what Lewis had done that he soon gave up trying to read the Narnia books and therefore didn't actually know them very well. He later admitted that they were outside his range of imaginative sympathy.

However, because Tolkien is now such a famous figure, his views have received a great deal of attention. Lots of people have drawn a sharp contrast between Tolkien's *The Lord of the Rings*, which is set in Middle-earth, and Lewis's Narnia. Middle-earth is obviously extremely detailed in every respect; it even has its own invented languages. Tolkien wanted it to have what he called "the inner consistency of reality." *The Lord of the Rings* was published with no fewer than *six* appendices!

Although Narnia doesn't have the same kind of obvious detail as Middle-earth, that doesn't necessarily mean it isn't detailed in its own way. The question we have to ask is, what *kind* of detail does it have? Did Lewis just throw in anything that struck his fancy, or was there a more careful intelligence at work?

It matters that we answer this question. Stories like Narnia deserve to be taken very seriously because what we read as children is perhaps the most important literature we ever encounter. We're then at a formative stage of life. "The hand that rocks the cradle is the hand that rules the world" goes the saying. And if that's true, what about the hand that holds the bedtime fairy-tale? For that matter, what about the hand that *writes* the bedtime fairy-tale?

C. S. Lewis, as a writer for children, shouldn't be dismissed with a casual wave of the hand. Since they were first published in the 1950s, his seven Chronicles of Narnia have been translated into more than thirty different languages and are now firmly established as classics of English literature. Walden Media's film version of *The Lion, the Witch and the Wardrobe* is one of the top-grossing movies ever made. If only because of Narnia's popularity, it matters that we understand what Lewis was up to.

As I got older and began to read his other writings, I became ever more intrigued by the seemingly random aspects to the Chronicles. They were not what you would expect of a man like Lewis with a highly trained mind. In his younger days he was tutored by a rigorous, logical thinker, William Kirkpatrick, who taught him that he should always have reasons for anything he said.

And it's easy to see that Lewis lapped up what Kirkpatrick taught him because randomness and mishmash are not to be found in his writings. Lewis is so famous as the author of Narnia that most people are unaware he had a day job. His career wasn't in writing children's books; it was in the world of academia. He taught for nearly thirty years at Oxford University and nearly ten at Cambridge University. It was his ability to think logically and express himself clearly that enabled him to have such a successful career as a university professor.

Lewis's field of academic interest was the literature of the Middle Ages and the Renaissance. He had a vast, specialized knowledge of European literary history, ranging across a thousand years up to about the year 1650. The biggest book he ever wrote was a massive doorstop of nearly seven hundred pages with the snappy title *English Literature in the Sixteenth Century Excluding Drama*. It was part of a multivolume series called the Oxford History of English Literature. Lewis took fifteen years to write it.

When I read Lewis's academic books, I noticed that he was a very careful writer, as a learned scholar ought to be. He didn't slop words together thoughtlessly but paid great attention to every single phrase he wrote. One of his closest friends, Owen Barfield, once said of Lewis that "what he thought about everything was secretly present in what he said about anything."

As a professor, Lewis enjoyed studying the works of old authors like Dante and Chaucer and Spenser, whose poems, so he said, "cannot be taken in at a glance." He added, "Everything leads to everything else, but by very intricate paths."

Lewis himself wrote a good deal of poetry. I am amazed by how complex it is. Many of his poems are almost impossibly intricate, and the subtlety of his word choice and rhyme schemes is simply jaw-dropping. He pointed out that the poems that look as if they have no special pattern are often the most complicated of all.

As for his views on fairy-tales, the same love of complexity was there, too. Lewis thought that the best fairy-tales have a very strict logic to them. They had to possess order and pattern or else they wouldn't please their readers. Just because a fairy-tale is full of magic and marvels doesn't mean that things can be "arbitrary," he said.

And what Lewis believed about the world of fairy-tales reflected his beliefs about the real world. As a Christian, he thought the universe had been made by God with very definite purposes. Even though the universe has been spoiled by sin, nevertheless God's plan is still being worked out. If only we had eyes to see it, we would notice the divine plan even in seemingly meaningless events—"the curve of every wave and the flight of every insect."

Lewis's view of fairy-tales sheds light on the Narnian mystery because it suggests that Lewis would have been very likely to write the Chronicles with *the most careful attention to detail*. The reason Father Christmas appears in *The Lion, the Witch and the Wardrobe* might not have been obvious to me. I might not have been able to explain the ways in which the books relate to the Bible. And yet that probably meant I was just too far away from Lewis's imagination to understand what he was doing. I was not properly tuned in to his wavelength.

The more I looked into this issue, the more I realized there was probably an inner meaning to the Narnia books even if I couldn't spot what it was. I felt rather like the Victorian astronomer John Couch Adams, who suspected the existence of the planet Neptune even before he actually observed it in the night sky.

Adams saw that there was a kink in the orbit of Uranus, which indicated there was a planet *beyond* Uranus, hidden from view but exerting the pull of gravity. A year *after* he realized this, Adams saw the mysterious planet through a telescope for the very first time. But he knew it existed before he observed it. (We will come back to Neptune in a later chapter because Lewis attached great importance to its discovery.)

The situation I was in reminded me not only of the search for the planet Neptune but also of what Lewis said about some of his favorite authors. He said each of their stories "at first looks planless, though all is planned." That was the Narnian mystery in a nutshell! It *looked* planless, but surely it was planned. The question I needed to answer about Narnia was this (please excuse the pun): did he or did he not plan it?

THE NARNIA CODE

Though many people have accepted the "hodgepodge" theory about the way Lewis wrote the Chronicles, there is another possible explanation. There might be a *secret* reason why Lewis retained Father Christmas, a *hidden* logic to his creative choices. Could Lewis have been following some underlying imaginative plan that he kept to himself? Was there perhaps a Narnia "code" waiting to be cracked?

The idea of secret codes usually makes people roll their eyes in disbelief—quite rightly, too, in most cases. When someone claims to have found a hidden code, it nearly always turns out to be a lot of nonsense. *The Da Vinci Code* is the most famous fictional example of this kind of far-fetched silliness.

And yet we shouldn't jump to a conclusion too quickly. Lewis was interested in codes. Many people know that he dedicated *The Lion, the Witch and the Wardrobe* to his goddaughter, Lucy Barfield, and named Lucy Pevensie after her. Hardly anyone knows that he had another god-child named Laurence Harwood and that Lewis often sent Laurence letters containing "puzzles to solve or secret writing to decode." (Harwood reprints these codes in his book, *C. S. Lewis, My Godfather*). The possibility that Narnia itself contains some kind of coded meaning is not a completely wild or crazy idea.

Lewis said that most of his books were written for *tous exo*, which is the Greek way of saying "those outside." He was referring to the passage in the Bible (quoted at the beginning of this chapter) in which Jesus said that He taught in parables so that "those outside" may be always seeing and never perceiving.

In other words, Jesus' stories needed to be decoded in order to be properly understood. Often, when He was alone with His disciples, Jesus explained the inner meaning of what He had said to the crowds. His parables are a prime example of coded language being used for a good purpose.

SUPPRESSED BY JACK

Assuming for a moment that Lewis *did* have a plan behind the series, is it really possible that he could have kept the plan to himself and told no one about it? Did he have the sort of personality that was capable of sitting on a big secret of this kind? Let us consider the evidence.

On the one hand, Lewis was an honest and straightforward man. He had a no-nonsense, down-to-earth attitude toward life, which went well with his self-chosen nickname, Jack. (He never liked his given names, Clive and Staples.) One of his closest friends, George Sayer, said that he and Jack talked together "in the frankest way as friends should" and that "I have never known a man more open about his private life."

On the other hand, Sayer also records the exact *opposite* about Lewis!

As well as remembering how open Lewis could be, Sayer said, "Jack never ceased to be secretive." Lewis could put up a smoke screen if he wanted to keep something private.

As a writer, Lewis sometimes wished to keep his own identity private. In order to do so, he used several different pen names in the course of his career.

One pen name was Clive Hamilton, which he used for the first two books he published. He gave one of these volumes to a friend without letting on that he himself was Clive Hamilton. The friend discovered it only later.

Another pen name was N. W. Clerk. *N. W.* stands for "Nat Whilk," the Anglo-Saxon way of saying, "I know not whom." *Clerk* means simply a writer or author. Altogether, then, *N. W. Clerk* means "a writer whom I don't know." Lewis used this name for one of his last books and was so keen to conceal his identity that he even disguised his style of writing.

But the most obvious and striking example of Lewis's secretiveness was when he got married and told no one what he had done. (This is what the film *Shadowlands* is all about.) He kept it secret for the best part of a year—an extraordinary thing to do! He even hid it from his good friend Tolkien. What is more surprising, would you say? To keep a marriage secret or to keep a literary code secret?

Speaking of surprises, Lewis wrote an autobiography called *Surprised by Joy*. It avoided mentioning so many important things that one of his friends joked a better title would have been *Suppressed by Jack!*

George Sayer remembered a time when he was out walking in the countryside with Lewis and they came across a bedraggled fox that was being chased by huntsmen with hounds. The fox ran off into a wood, and then the huntsmen rode up on their horses. Lewis shouted out to the first riders, "'Hallo, yoicks, gone that way,' and pointed to the direction opposite to the one the fox had taken. The whole hunt followed his directions."

All these things show that Lewis was capable of keeping secrets, sometimes very major secrets (such as his marriage), and that he didn't mind misleading people if he thought there was good reason to do so.

The more I found out about his personality, the more I suspected there was a hidden meaning to Narnia.

EUREKA!

Reading what other people had written about Lewis and Narnia, I noticed that I wasn't the only person with this suspicion. Lots of people who have studied the Chronicles and their author have asked themselves, "There's more going on here than meets the eye. But what *is* it?"

Many different answers have been suggested.

One scholar tried to show that the seven Narnia stories are linked to the classical virtues (faith, hope, love, justice, prudence, temperance, and courage).

Another couple of scholars took the exact opposite approach and suggested that Narnia's unifying theme was the seven deadly sins (lust, gluttony, greed, sloth, anger, envy, and pride).

Numerous other ideas have been put forward, such as the seven sacraments and the seven sections of Spenser's *Faerie Queene* (a poem Lewis loved), but none of these ideas proved to be the solution to the riddle.

I myself once made a halfhearted attempt to link the Chronicles with different plays by Shakespeare, but I soon abandoned it. I knew I was just twisting the Chronicles to fit in with my own thinking.

And so the years went by. While I was a student at Oxford University, I occasionally thought about this mystery, trying out one idea and then another—without any success. I steadily read more and more of Lewis's works, teaching and lecturing and writing about them. I even lived for three years in what had been his Oxford home, The Kilns, working there as a warden and curator, sleeping in Lewis's old bedroom and studying in his study.

Then I moved to Cambridge and began to write a doctoral thesis on his imagination. One night, when I was thirty-five years old and lying in bed in my college room, just about to go to sleep, I had a thought. I sat up in bed and said to myself, *That's it! I've got it!*

The mystery was solved. I had cracked the Narnia code.

CHAPTER TWO

THE BEAM OF LIGHT

In Your light we see light.
PSALM 36:9

GOOD IDEAS COME when you're relaxed and not thinking too hard. They tend to happen in one of the three Bs—the bed, the bus, or the bath. One of the most famous moments of inspiration is said to have occurred to the ancient Greek thinker Archimedes while he was sitting in his bath. He was so excited by his idea that he ran naked down the street shouting "eureka" ("I've found it!") at the top of his lungs.

My breakthrough was considerably less important than that of Archimedes, but it thrilled me just as much (or so I guess). Fortunately for my neighbors, I didn't run naked down the street, but I did jump from my bed and begin to pull Lewis's books off my shelves, chasing the idea from work to work.

Before I jumped out of bed, what had I been thinking about?

I'm afraid you'll have to wait until the next chapter to read about that. There was a clue in the last chapter when I asked, "Did he or did he not plan it?" but we won't follow up on that clue until chapter 3.

As I mentioned in chapter 1, my own eureka moment was preceded by years of studying Lewis's worldview. In this chapter, I want to pass on some key insights into how Lewis thought, which will help you better understand why I believe in the Narnia code.

The first thing to understand is that Lewis believed the human mind worked in two ways—through "Enjoyment" and through "Contemplation." The difference between these two ways of knowing was *massively* important to Lewis. Once we grasp what he meant by Enjoyment and Contemplation, we will more easily be able to see why he wrote the Narnia Chronicles the way he did.

And in order to understand what Lewis meant by Enjoyment and Contemplation, we need to accompany him, not to his study or his library, but to his garden shed, where he liked to go and think deep thoughts.

"MEDITATION IN A TOOLSHED"

Lewis was standing in the darkness of his toolshed one sunny day. It was bright outside but dark inside, and through a crack at the top of the door he could see a beam of sunlight slanting down through the darkness of the shed. He could see little particles of dust floating in the beam, which lit up a small patch of the floor.

Then he shifted his position so that the beam of light was no longer falling on the floor: it was now falling directly on his eyes. And instantly the previous picture vanished. He no longer saw the beam of light. It had disappeared from view. He saw *along* the beam of light. And what he saw along it was the crack at the top of the door, the leaves on the tree moving in the wind outside, and millions of miles away, the sun itself.

Looking at the beam and looking along the beam are very different experiences.

Lewis's point in his "Meditation in a Toolshed" (the title of the essay where he wrote about this memory) is that we should consider every question in both ways—both by "looking at" it and by "looking along" it.

For instance, take falling in love. Why do people fall in love with each other and get married and have children? The biologist might say it's because we want to pass on our genes to the next generation and ensure the survival of the species. The sociologist might say that it's because there are certain social structures and expectations that shape the way we behave.

But if you asked a particular man why he had fallen in love with a particular woman, he wouldn't say anything like that. Instead, he would probably say, "I love her because—um, ah, er—because I love her! Time seems to stand still when I'm with her. She's the best thing that ever happened to me. I want to be with her all the time. And anyway, she laughs at my jokes!"

Whose opinion is the most reliable? The opinion of the scientists who are contemplating, or looking at, the lovers? Or the opinion of the couple themselves, who are enjoying love, looking along the beam of their love?

"Looking at" and "looking along" are both valuable in different ways, and we shouldn't automatically assume that one is necessarily better or worse than the other. In certain cases we may have good reason to prefer one way, but generally we should be willing to consider every question in both lights.

Lewis jokingly said we should be like the ancient Persians who debated everything twice: once when they were sober and once when they were drunk! Of course, he wasn't literally suggesting that drunkenness is a good thing, but he was suggesting that we can see certain things only when we are immersed in an experience, enjoying and looking *along* it, committed to it, living within it.

And the interesting thing about the experience of looking along is that the beam of light becomes *invisible*. You no longer see the light; you see *by* it. The beam itself vanishes from your sight.

Lewis writes about this idea not only in his "Toolshed" essay, but also in a fable he wrote in his twenties called "The Man Born Blind."

"THE MAN BORN BLIND"

This short story is about a man named Robin, blind from birth, who regains his sight after an operation. When the bandages are removed from his eyes, Robin expects to see the wonderful thing he has heard about all his life—light. But no one can show it to him. He asks his wife, Mary, to tell him where it is, and she can't explain. Her attempts to do so only confuse him further.

At first Mary says that the light is "all round us," and Robin wonders therefore whether light is everything he can see. Then Mary narrows it down to the lightbulb hanging from the ceiling. Then she corrects herself and says that the light is what comes from the bulb, it's not the bulb itself. But, she adds, the room is very light even when the light isn't switched on. She points at things that are *in* the light or have a lovely light *on* them, and the more she tries to explain things clearly, the more Robin thinks he will never understand. Why is light so complicated and confusing? All he wants to do is to see the light! Is that too much to ask?

In his frustration, he leaves the house and walks up to the little cliff next to the local quarry, where the rising sun is burning through the morning mist. On the cliff edge Robin finds an artist who is standing in front of an easel, painting. The artist points to the golden mist swirling in the quarry beneath them and says he is trying to catch the light before it goes. The next moment the artist is alone on the quarry edge. Robin has taken a dive into the bright fog and has fallen to his death.

That's all there is to this story. It's very short and ends suddenly without any explanation. However, in many other places Lewis talked about the point of the story, which is simply this: *Light is not something you see; it's something you see by.*

Robin didn't realize that light, though it makes everything else visible, is itself invisible. He thought he would be able to get inside the light by diving into the shining mist, when in fact the light was *already* inside him, enabling him to see the mist in the first place.

He was already looking *along* light; there was no way he could look *at* it. If he stepped outside light in order to look back at it, he would have no light to see it by! To express this idea in other terms that Lewis sometimes used: Robin was *enjoying* light while foolishly trying to *contemplate* it instead.

Grasping this difference between Enjoyment and Contemplation was a great breakthrough for Lewis. He described it as "an indispensable tool of thought." He realized—and he never forgot—that there are some things that can only be fully known from the inside.

Two things in particular are much better known from the inside (Enjoyment) than the outside (Contemplation), and it is vital that we spend some time discussing both these things in order to understand what Lewis was up to when he wrote the Narnia Chronicles.

The first thing that we know much better from the inside than from the outside is God.

IN GOD'S LIGHT WE SEE LIGHT

Imagine you're a writer like C. S. Lewis and you want to write a series of stories "about Christ." How would you tackle this task?

If you're like me, you would invent some kind of Christlike character who goes about doing Christlike things: loving people, forgiving people, teaching them, suffering for them, and so on. And that would be a good and biblical way of writing the story.

But it would also leave out a big part of the biblical picture because, according to the New Testament, Christ is much more than a solitary historical figure moving about the world doing things to people. He's the one who made the world! He's the Son of God; He is God the Son, the divine Word by whom all things were made. To quote the apostle Paul: "All things were created by him [Christ] and for him . . . and in him all things hold together" (Colossians 1:16-17, NIV).

This scriptural passage was of great interest to C. S. Lewis. He liked it so much that he wrote his own paraphrase of it: "[Christ] is the all-pervasive principle of concretion or cohesion whereby the universe holds together." In other words, Christ is the cosmic glue that keeps all the parts of creation in place.

Now, how would you get *that* aspect of Christ—the One who is the glue holding everything together—into your story? How would you show the glue without showing everything it glues?

And the difficulty gets even worse! Because *all* things hold together in Christ, *our very understanding* of Christ is held together in Him. We can't, in that sense, step outside Him and look back *at* Him as if from some spectator's point of view. We're already "in Christ" because He has made us and is keeping us in existence from moment to moment. He glues our minds and our thoughts together just as much as He glues everything else.

Interestingly, that is the case even if we're not Christians. Even non-Christians owe their whole being to God, including their ability to dis-believe in Him! If non-Christians become Christians, they then become "in Christ" in another sense—voluntarily, through faith and obedience. But everyone already knows the divine nature at the most basic level because God is everyone's Creator.

And that puts us all into something of a predicament. Although we can step outside of God's will by rebelling against Him, we can't step outside Him altogether. If we could do *that*, we would cease to exist! We're already in Christ as His creatures whether we like it or not. We've never known a moment when He wasn't our Creator, ensuring our existence.

In one of his books, Lewis put it like this: "We may ignore, but we can nowhere evade, the presence of God. The world is crowded with Him. He walks everywhere *incognito*."

In another place, Lewis wrote:

> The fact which is in one respect the most obvious and primary fact, and through which alone you have access to all the other facts, may be precisely the one that is most easily forgotten— forgotten not because it is so remote or abstruse but because it is so near and so obvious. And that is exactly how the Supernatural has been forgotten.

In other words, it's a bit like people who live next door to railway stations and who don't notice the noise of the trains. They've become so used to the noise that they now don't hear it. They miss it not because it's not there, but because it's everywhere: their whole world is full of the sound of trains! They have no negative with which to contrast their positive experience of this noise. Because they've never been aware of its absence, they've ceased to be aware of its presence.

The answer to this problem is not to try to find a negative—not to try to live without God in order to find out what living with Him is like. The answer is to become alive to the reality of our situation—to wake up and to realize that God is *already* in the world and in our lives, in the workings of our mind, in the faces of those we meet, in the breath of our lungs, in the light of our eyes. God has to be there, because "in him all things hold together." As King David said in Psalm 36:9, "In Your light we see light."

The main way we know God as Christians, Lewis thought, is through *enjoying* Him, not *contemplating* Him. It's a bit like a relationship with another human being. The best way to get to know someone is not to read facts about them on Wikipedia or look at their photos on Facebook. The best way to get to know someone is to actually live with them. By living with someone, you don't just know *about* that person, you *know* them.

Lewis believed that coming to know God is much more like "breathing a new atmosphere" than it is like "learning a subject." You can't examine God from the outside as you would study a figure from history or follow a character in a TV series. Or perhaps you *can*, but it's not going to make you much the wiser! It would be like examining raindrops on a window in order to quench your thirst.

How do these things relate to the Narnia code, the inner meaning of the Chronicles? That question brings us to the second of the two things that are better known from the inside than from the outside. The first thing is God; the second thing is the world of a story.

KRYPTONITE

Several years before he published the Narnia books, Lewis gave a talk called "The Kappa Element in Romance."

Kappa is the initial letter of the Greek word *krypton*, meaning cryptic or hidden, and *Romance* means a fairy-tale or an adventure story. (So "The Kappa Element in Romance" basically means "The Hidden Element in Story." *The Hidden Element in Story!* It's a pretty clear sign that Lewis was interested in literary secrets!)

In his talk, Lewis said that stories contain many things we value only if they remain hidden: these include "the mystery of life" and the unexpected "twist" that sometimes comes at the end of a story. An author can't flag these things without ruining the very effect for which he is aiming.

Lewis later rewrote "The Kappa Element in Romance" as the essay "On Stories." In this essay he talks about one particular cryptic thing that he thought was more important than any other. He calls it the "atmosphere" or general feel of a story.

The example he uses to explain what he means is taken from the great American novel *The Last of the Mohicans*, written by James Fenimore Cooper, which has been made into an Oscar-winning film.

The Last of the Mohicans includes a moment of great suspense when the hero is half asleep by his fire in the woods while a Native American warrior is silently creeping toward him with a tomahawk in his hand.

What if this warrior had been carrying a pistol rather than a tomahawk? It would ruin the whole scene, Lewis says. The scene plunges the reader into the Native American world, a world of snowshoes, canoes, wigwams, feathered headdresses, war paint, whiskered trousers—and, yes, tomahawks, not pistols. Pistols don't belong there, and they would change the whole atmosphere of the book if Fenimore Cooper had decided to include them.

The point Lewis is trying to make is that the atmosphere of this scene is just as important as the threat it poses to the hero. A pistol would probably have put the hero in much greater danger than a tomahawk, but the *level* of danger doesn't matter. What matters is the *kind* of danger. The kind of danger represented by a tomahawk is different from that represented by a gun.

A good writer won't just give you a rollicking plot and crank up the tension by any old means. A good writer gives you the flavor or feel of a whole world.

Here's another example. Lewis imagines telling a "Martian" story— that is, a story set on the planet Mars. How would you go about it? Well, you would need to use "Martianity" throughout, he says. You wouldn't use Mars just for the location and Martians for the characters. "Martianity" would have to be woven into the whole story, "emotionally and atmospherically *as well as* logically" so that the story would hang together and feel coherent and united. You couldn't just relocate a Wild West story or a New York crime story to another planet. A truly Martian adventure would welcome you into its own story world, with its own definite flavor or quality.

The way to test which books have a good flavor, Lewis says, is to ask which books you reread. Having read a book once, you know the plot, so you know what's going to happen. Then why bother to read it again? You bother to read it again if you *enjoy the atmosphere*. You like being part of that imagined world. You can't be surprised by the events of the story, but you can be enthralled by its taste. In that sense, the atmosphere is much more important than the plot.

Some stories are all plot and no atmosphere. The example Lewis gives is *The Three Musketeers*. He thought it was a bad book because it had no "weather" or color to it. The characters go from London to Paris, but there's no sense that Paris is any different from London. You might read *The Three Musketeers* once in order to find out what happens at the end. But you probably wouldn't read it a second time.

When Lewis began writing the Narnia Chronicles, he wanted to avoid the pitfalls of *The Three Musketeers* and imitate the example of *The Last of the Mohicans*. He was interested in telling stories with an atmosphere—and in order to make that atmosphere convincing, every single element had to fit. Even the smallest details mattered.

Lewis wrote:

A child is always thinking about those details in a story which a grown-up regards as indifferent. If when you first told the tale your hero was warned by three little men appearing on the left of the road, and when you tell it again you introduce one little man on the right of the road, the child protests. And the child is right. You think it makes no difference because you are not living the story at all. If you were, you would know better.

When we "live the story," we get completely wrapped up in it so that every detail becomes important. If you change the details, you ruin the magic—the magic illusion that you're in another world with its own kind of oxygen.

And the odd thing about the atmosphere of a good story is that, although you come to know it, you don't notice it. It is effectively hidden from you because it's everywhere you look. Here is yet another example of looking along the beam!

We can think of a story's atmosphere in the same way we think of Earth's atmosphere—the literal atmosphere that is made up mostly of nitrogen and oxygen. We breathe this atmosphere. You have taken several breaths of it even while you've been reading this page. But did you notice you were doing so? I expect not.

Unless the atmosphere is poisoned in some way (by cigarette smoke, for example) or unless we've failed to take enough breaths (which might cause us to faint), we usually never think about the air we breathe. It surrounds us. It's the element we live in, and we give it a second thought only when it goes wrong or we treat it in the wrong way.

The same holds true for the atmospheres of stories. When the author has successfully woven a story-world together, we accept that all its different parts belong naturally in the same tale. Its individual parts stick out only when the author has made a mistake or when we don't fully understand the atmosphere. "As is proper in romance, the inner meaning is carefully hidden," as Lewis said in reference to a story he once wrote.

And this is where we come back to Father Christmas in *The Lion, the*

Witch and the Wardrobe. As a child, I thought Father Christmas stuck out like a sore thumb. But did he stick out because Lewis had made a mistake or because I had failed to breathe the atmosphere of the book properly?

In other words, was Lewis a bad writer, or was I a bad reader?

To answer that question, we must return to my eureka moment in bed. . . .

CHAPTER THREE

THE SEVEN HEAVENS

The heavens are telling the glory of God.

PSALM 19:1

MY EUREKA MOMENT HAPPENED not in the bath, as was the case with Archimedes, but in my bed. It was nearly midnight one Wednesday in February. At the time I was reading something that had no connection with Narnia—at least on the face of it.

It was a long poem called "The Planets." Lewis wrote it in 1935, fifteen years before he published the first Chronicle, *The Lion, the Witch and the Wardrobe.* I was just about to close the book and turn the light off when, all of a sudden, the light went on. A different light—the light of understanding.

"The Planets" poem is all about how the planets were understood in medieval times, when it was believed there were only seven planets and that they exerted influences over the Earth, affecting people, events, and even the metals in the Earth's crust.

Few people today think the planets exert influences, but every time anyone mentions falling ill with the flu (influenza) they are referring back to that idea without realizing it. In the Middle Ages, it was thought that the planets influenced people by affecting the air of Earth's atmosphere. If a doctor couldn't explain an illness, he would probably say, "It's caused by the influence in the air right now." If he was an Italian doctor, he would not say *influence*, but *influenza*. The word found its way into English medical dictionaries, and we still use it!

According to astronomers in the Middle Ages, each planet exerted its own special *influenza*. Mars, being associated with war, would turn you into a "martial" warrior. Venus, the planet of love, would help you find your sweetheart. Mercury produced the metal mercury (quicksilver) on Earth. The other planets influenced Earth in yet other ways.

BY JOVE, I'VE GOT IT!

The part of the poem that made me do a double take was the section dealing with Jupiter (also known as Jove). Jupiter, according to the poem, influenced the Earth by bringing about:

> . . . *winter passed*
> *And guilt forgiven.*

Those five words leaped off the page at me. I rubbed my eyes. "Winter passed and guilt forgiven"? I had come across those two things in another of Lewis's works. The passing of winter and the forgiving of guilt are two of the main events in *The Lion, the Witch and the Wardrobe*. The White Witch's winter passes, and Edmund's guilt is forgiven. This little phrase seemed like a five-word summary of the first Narnia story.

I looked more closely at the lines dealing with Jupiter and its influences. A suspiciously large amount of the imagery in the poem seemed to link up with things in *The Lion, the Witch and the Wardrobe*. It mentioned kings and the lionhearted and royal robes and rulers who were "just and gentle" (like King Edmund the Just and Queen Susan the Gentle). Could I possibly, after all these years, have stumbled upon Lewis's secret code?

I then looked at the sections in the poem dealing with the other six medieval planets. I could see that the other six Chronicles seemed to be summarized there too: one Chronicle for each planet.

I was stunned. How could no one have seen this before? It was so obvious once I noticed it! I spent the next two weeks walking around the University of Cambridge in a daze, hardly able to believe what had fallen in my lap.

Naturally, I had to set aside all the work I'd been doing on my thesis up to that point. This was too big an idea not to explore as fully as I possibly could. I devoted all of the next year to rereading absolutely everything Lewis had ever written. I wanted to check and double-check and triple-check this theory, because, if it turned out to be true, I knew lots of people were going to be interested.

And the more I examined the evidence, the more it showed itself to be correct. I became convinced this wasn't just a theory; it was a genuine discovery.

I then spent the next four years writing a big, fat book about it! This book that you're now holding in your hands, *The Narnia Code*, is the younger brother of that big, fat book. If you want to find further information about anything you read here, please take a look at the much more detailed account I give in *Planet Narnia: The Seven Heavens in the Imagination of C. S. Lewis* (New York: Oxford University Press, 2008).

IN 1543, COPERNICUS CHANGED THE SKY WE SEE

Perhaps you're asking, *Aren't there more than seven planets?* Yes, indeed, there are these days, according to modern astronomers. But here is where we need to do a little history.

Back in the Middle Ages, the period that Lewis was such an expert on, astronomers believed they had identified seven planets. They included the Sun and the Moon (odd as that now seems to us), as well as Mercury, Venus, Mars, Jupiter, and Saturn.

Each of these seven planets could be seen wandering alone across the sky. (The Greek word for "wanderers" is *planetai*.) During the day, the Sun took its solitary course from east to west, and during the night the other six "planets" wended their way across the sky, following their own unique paths.

Before the invention of the telescope in about 1610, these were the only seven objects that could be seen wandering about the sky. All the other heavenly bodies were not lonely *planetai* but stars, either fixed in position like the North Star or members of groups (constellations) that all moved together as one.

Not until 1781 was the planet Uranus identified by an astronomer using a telescope. Neptune was discovered in 1846—although, as I mentioned in the first chapter, John Couch Adams realized that Neptune existed even before he actually observed it. (We'll come back to Neptune at the end of this book.) Pluto was discovered in 1930 and was included in the standard list of planets until 2006, when the International Astronomical Union decided it should be classified as a dwarf planet.

But for many thousands of years before the invention of the telescope, when you had to scour the heavens with your naked eye, there was no Uranus, no Neptune, no Pluto, and—most bizarrely—no Earth!

Earth was not considered a planet in those days because people believed that the Earth was fixed at the very center of the universe.

Therefore, it did no wandering. The Earth didn't go round the Sun: the Sun went round the Earth.

Everyone thought this way until 1543, when Polish astronomer and canon of Frauenburg Cathedral Nicholas Copernicus wondered whether the Sun, rather than the Earth, might be the center of the universe. Copernicus published his theory in a book called *On the Revolutions of the Heavenly Spheres.*

His theory was a revolution in its own right. It has been described as the biggest change ever in the history of human thought. Until Copernicus's time, the Earth was viewed as the center of everything. After Copernicus, the Earth was on the sidelines, and the Sun was at the center. You could say that, in a sense, Copernicus single-handedly moved the whole Earth! Following the Copernican Revolution, astronomy became divided into two great epochs: the pre-Copernican and the post-Copernican. Before. And after.

C. S. Lewis was fascinated by the Copernican Revolution because it happened during the century he studied so much. Lewis's book *English Literature in the Sixteenth Century Excluding Drama* opens with a long discussion of the "new astronomy."

Lewis points out that the universe as it was understood in pre-Copernican times was "tingling with life," whereas in post-Copernican times the universe is thought of more like a machine. When Lewis says the universe was "tingling," he is having a private joke. The Old English word *tingul* means "star," and usually when Lewis uses the word *tingle* or *tingling*, he is suggesting something special about the stars. (Look for further references to tingling later in this book.)

The title of another of Lewis's academic works, *The Discarded Image*, refers to the pre-Copernican "image," or model, of the universe, which, of course, was gradually discarded as Copernicus's theory was explored, tested, and eventually proved correct by the Christian astronomer Galileo.

But although this image was discarded once it was disproven scientifically, Lewis thought it was vital we remember it; otherwise, we would cut ourselves off from our own past. We need to know where we've come from in order to know where we are. Having an accurate knowledge of history (including the history of science) helps save us from making certain mistakes in the modern day. For instance, how old is space?

A WASTE OF SPACE

If I told you that space is less than four hundred years old, you would think I was crazy. Well, here goes: Space is a good deal less than four hundred years old.

Am I crazy? No! Astronomers didn't use the word *space* in this sense until the seventeenth century. Before then they used other words such as *firmament* and *heavens*. In *The Discarded Image*, Lewis points out how different we would feel if we took a walk under the sky at night and looked up at the planets believing that pre-Copernican astronomy was actually correct. We would feel as if we were looking *into* the heavens. These days, with our modern astronomical beliefs, we feel as if we're looking *out* at the blackness of empty space.

There is a big difference between "space" and "the heavens." *Space* suggests a shapeless emptiness in which Earth has no particular seat of honor. Earth is now just one of many planets, endlessly revolving around a not-very-special star that we call the Sun. In that sense, modern space is a kind of chaos or wilderness as far as Earth is concerned.

But before Copernicus, Earth was securely located in its own very special place. Earth was not just another wanderer in empty space but the fixed heart of an intricately patterned cosmos.

The word *cosmos* comes from a Greek word meaning "to organize, to arrange." It's where we get the word *cosmetics*. When a woman applies cosmetics to her face—lipstick, eyeliner, blush—she is bringing out the shape and the pattern of her facial features, "organizing" her appearance to make it look more attractive.

Cosmologists bring out the shape and the pattern of the universe, as they believe that shape and pattern to be. And before the time of Copernicus, cosmologists thought that not only was the Earth at the center—the focus of every created thing—but also that it was surrounded by a series of heavens or transparent spheres. The universe was a bit like a gigantic onion, with Earth being the middle of the onion and the heavens being the rings surrounding that central core.

There were seven heavens, and each heaven had a different planet rotating within it. So instead of formless and vacant space, there was a series of spheres, one inside the other (rather like Russian nesting dolls) all the way up to the edge of the created order.

The pre-Copernican list of the seven planets runs like this (in their supposed order from the static and central Earth):

1. Moon
2. Mercury
3. Venus
4. Sun
5. Mars
6. Jupiter
7. Saturn

The diagram on page 149 illustrates this arrangement.

Occasionally you still hear people say of something that has made them very happy, "I was in the seventh heaven!" It would be delightful to be in the seventh heaven, according to pre-Copernican ways of thinking, because there you would be in the planetary sphere farthest from Earth and nearest the home of God, outside the created order altogether.

SEVEN DEITIES A WEEK

In pre-Copernican times, Christians believed (as we still believe) that God ruled the universe. But as Lewis explains in *The Discarded Image*, medieval Christians believed that, in addition to man, God had made spirits of various kinds, sometimes called gods, deities, intelligences, or angels, to have authority under Him. Today, Christians often talk about angels but tend to avoid using the word *gods*, assuming that it can refer only to "pagan gods." However, the Bible itself sometimes uses the word *gods* without referring to something occultic or evil. The most obvious place is in John 10:34-36, where Jesus quotes Psalm 82:6 ("Is it not written in your law, 'I said, you are gods'?").

Medieval Christians believed that not only had God created these various spirits but that He had put seven of them in charge of the seven planets. Each planet was governed by its own god or angel, who in turn ruled over a different day of the week. Saturn ruled Saturday. The Sun ruled Sunday. The Moon ruled Monday.

You'll be able to work out how the remaining four days of the week relate to the other four planets if you know French or Spanish. Mars provides the name for Tuesday, which is called *Mardi* in French and *Martes* in Spanish. Even in English we sometimes talk about *Mardi Gras* (Shrove Tuesday), the day before the beginning of Lent. The Norse equivalent of the Roman Mars is Tyr or Tiw, and so we get the name *Tues*day.

Mercury is the planet for Wednesday, which is called *Mercredi* in French and *Miercoles* in Spanish. The Norse version of Mercury is Woden, and so we say *Wednes*day in English. Thursday's planet was Jupiter (or Jove), and Thursday is *Jeudi* in French and *Jueves* in Spanish. The Norse version of Jupiter is Thor, giving us *Thurs*day. And Friday's planet was Venus, Friday being *Vendredi* in French and *Viernes* in Spanish. The Norse equivalent of Venus is Freya or Frigg (*Fri*day).

So, in fact, we refer to this sevenfold system of the planets every day of our lives! Most of us have forgotten the connection, if we ever knew it. And yet C. S. Lewis was very much alive to this old tradition because of his work studying the literature of the Middle Ages and the Renaissance. Let's not forget, that was his professional career. It was what he was paid to think about. It should come as no surprise to us that Lewis knew a great deal about this old image of the universe, with Earth at the center, which so influenced the poems, plays, and myths he studied as a professor.

Many of the old writers Lewis studied took the planetary gods and used them as symbols for God. As Lewis notes, "Gods and goddesses could always be used in a Christian sense." In fact, in Shakespeare's time, writers *had* to use the gods when talking about God. An Act of Parliament in 1606 made it illegal to utter God's name on the stage, so Shakespeare started using the names of the planetary gods, particularly that of Jupiter (or Jove), whenever one of his characters needed to mention God. Lewis commented, "The gods are God incognito and everyone is in the secret."

But Lewis didn't just study this old system of the cosmos and the way writers used it symbolically. He also loved it! He wrote in *The Discarded Image*:

> I have made no serious effort to hide the fact that the old Model delights me as I believe it delighted our ancestors. Few constructions of the imagination seem to me to have combined splendour, sobriety, and coherence in the same degree. It is possible that some readers have long been itching to remind me that it had a serious defect; it was not true.
>
> I agree. It was not true.

Nevertheless, Lewis valued the model very highly. Why?

GOOD HEAVENS ABOVE

There are three main reasons why Lewis loved the pre-Copernican cosmos.

The first is that many of his favorite poets from medieval times loved it. The most famous poem in which this old cosmos appears is *The Divine Comedy* by the Italian poet Dante (1265–1321). In the final part of *The Divine Comedy* the main character climbs up through the seven heavens in his ascent to God's throne. Lewis hugely admired this poem and described it as "the highest point that poetry had ever reached." We will mention *The Divine Comedy* again in chapter 10.

A second reason Lewis loved this old astronomy is because the seven planets provided a set of colorful and meaningful symbols. The meanings that people attached to each of the planets weren't dreamed up out of nowhere. You can see how the Sun, because of its color, would have become associated with gold and therefore with riches—not just money, but also mental and spiritual wealth. Accordingly, the Sun was thought to play a role in making people into philosophers and theologians.

Venus, which is especially beautiful, became a symbol of all that is most pure and lovely. I remember the first time I knew I was looking at Venus. It was early one morning, just after dawn, and someone pointed out to me what looked like a huge diamond glittering above the horizon. It's no surprise that "the Morning Star"—one of Venus's names—is used in the Bible as a way of describing Jesus Christ (see, e.g., 2 Peter 1:19).

The silvery Moon—also known as Luna—became linked to mental instability because of the way that the Moon changes shape and size and moves about the sky so quickly, disappearing totally once every month. A "lunatic" was someone under the influence of Luna.

Gradually over the centuries, all seven planets had meanings attached to them. C. S. Lewis viewed these meanings as permanently valuable. And he was right. Even today you can still see them being used as symbols. I recently watched a film called *The Madness of King George* and noticed how the director had deliberately included a huge bright moon in one particular scene as a way of showing that King George III had become a lunatic. Perhaps it was the loss of the American colonies that tipped him into insanity. . . .

In the next seven chapters, I will take you through the seven planets and their meanings and show you how (so I believe) C. S. Lewis constructed each Narnia Chronicle out of these ancient symbolic associations.

But before we start that process, let me mention one last reason why Lewis particularly loved the pre-Copernican cosmos. It relates to what I just said about Venus being an image of the beauty of Jesus Christ, a picture of the divine.

Lewis thought that pre-Copernican astronomy was in some ways a more complete kind of science than modern astronomy. That's because the old model was interested in the idea of spiritual meanings and qualities in the universe.

Modern astronomy tends to look at the universe as a machine that obeys the impersonal laws of physics. We now usually think of the stars and planets in a materialistic way—made up of so much carbon, nitrogen, or other chemical material.

In the older view, the universe was viewed more like a body, or an organism, with its own intentions and spiritual significance. In those days, the planets moved (so it was thought) like birds flying away from and then back toward their nests. These days scientists consider planetary movements to be more like cogs in a clockwork mechanism. "The 'space' of modern astronomy," Lewis said, "may arouse terror, or bewilderment or vague reverie; the spheres of the old [astronomy] present us with an object in which the mind can rest, overwhelming in its greatness but satisfying in its harmony."

Both ways of thinking have value. But Lewis thought the older view was especially worth remembering because it allowed scientists to think about qualities as well as quantities when they investigated things. Consider the way the star Ramandu gently rebukes Eustace in *The Voyage of the "Dawn Treader."* Eustace is surprised to meet a literal star and tells him, "In our world a star is a huge ball of flaming gas." Ramandu replies, "Even in your world, my son, that is not what a star is but only what it is made of."

The point Lewis is trying to make is that we shouldn't reduce stars to their physical parts. If we do, we will have lost something of the truth. A fuller picture of the truth is to be found in the Bible's way of viewing the heavens—and that's what we'll look at now in the final sections of this chapter.

THE HEAVENS ARE TELLING THE GLORY OF GOD

From the very start of the Bible, the stars have great significance. In the Creation story, we're told that God creates the stars "for signs and for seasons." God makes the sun to "rule the day" and the moon to "rule the night" (Genesis 1:14, 16).

These heavenly bodies have a purpose: they indicate "days and years." A day, obviously, is the period between one sunrise and the next. A month (a lunar month) is the period between one new moon and the next. A year is the time it takes for the sun to return to rising from the same point in the east.

But as well as signifying periods of time, the starry heavens signify other things too. The "morning stars sang together" when God created the world (Job 38:7). And one special star sang a very special message, as recorded in the Gospel of Matthew:

Now when Jesus was born in Bethlehem of Judea in the days
of Herod the king, behold, wise men from the East came to
Jerusalem, saying, "Where is he who has been born king of the

Jews? For we have seen his star in the East, and have come to worship him." . . . And lo, the star which they had seen in the East went before them, till it came to rest over the place where the child was. When they saw the star, they rejoiced exceedingly with great joy; and going into the house they saw the child with Mary his mother, and they fell down and worshiped him. Then, opening their treasures, they offered him gifts, gold and frankincense and myrrh. (Matthew 2:1-2, 9-11)

The Star of Bethlehem led the wise men to Jesus. It was a guide, a signpost. And this should not surprise us, because in the Psalms we read that "the heavens are telling the glory of God" (Psalm 19:1). Echoing verse 4 of Psalm 19, the apostle Paul seems to say that the heavens do not just tell the glory of God; they speak the word of Christ (Romans 10:18).

In the book of Judges, the stars are portrayed as angels who can act in human affairs. The Israelites were oppressed for twenty years by a man called Sisera, commander of the armies of Canaan, who was eventually defeated because, according to the song of Deborah, "the stars in their courses fought against Sisera" (Judges 5:20, KJV). Lewis refers to this verse in his book *Out of the Silent Planet,* one of three novels he wrote about interplanetary adventures.

Many centuries after Sisera, Jesus pointed to the stars and warned people to look up at the heavens if they wished to know when the time of tribulation would come: "[In] those days the sun will be darkened, and the moon will not give its light, and the stars will fall from heaven, and the powers of the heavens will be shaken; then will appear the sign of the Son of man in heaven" (Matthew 24:29-30).

And in Revelation, the apostle John writes about a vision he had in which he saw the Son of Man holding "the seven stars in his right hand" (Revelation 1:16, 20; 2:1). What is meant by these seven stars? One suggestion is that these seven stars referred to the seven wandering stars, the planets. As already pointed out, there has been a special connection between the seven planets and the seven days of the week since the earliest recorded history. If this is a correct way of understanding Revelation, Christ is being shown as the Lord of time, holding all the days of our lives in His hands. Lewis's good friend Austin Farrer, who was a biblical scholar, interpreted the verse in this way.

Throughout the Bible, then, we see that the stars have meanings and qualities that can be studied for good and godly purposes. And it is very important to remember all these things whenever C. S. Lewis mentions that easily misunderstood word *astrology*.

WISE MEN AND THE STARS

What is astrology? Many people, especially Christian people, think astrology is at best foolish and at worst very dangerous. These days astrology is connected with silly horoscopes in the back pages of magazines. Astrology in that sense is superstitious nonsense and has nothing to do with astrology as Lewis meant it.

Lewis understood astrology in the same way that he understood biology or geology. In biology you study *bios*—the Greek word for life. In geology you study *ge*—the Greek word for the Earth. And in astrology, you study the *astral* bodies, the stars.

Astrology means "study of the stars," and astronomy means "law of the stars." The two branches of study were intermingled in pre-Copernican times. Lewis explains it this way:

> The spheres transmit (to the Earth) what are called
> Influences—the subject-matter of Astrology. Astrology is
> not specifically medieval. The Middle Ages inherited it
> from antiquity and bequeathed it to the Renaissance. The
> statement that the medieval Church frowned upon this

discipline is often taken in a sense that makes it untrue. Orthodox theologians could accept the theory that the planets had an effect on events and on psychology and, much more, on plants and minerals.

Lewis is then quick to explain that the medieval church absolutely opposed astrology if it led people to worship the planets and if it was used for "the lucrative, and politically undesirable, practice of astrologically grounded predictions." The church also opposed astrology where it led to determinism, for while Christians until the time of Copernicus generally believed that the stars influenced us, they didn't think the stars *controlled* us. The stars might give a disposition or a tendency, but they couldn't overrule a person's free will and responsibility before God. In many ways, those living in medieval times thought of stars much as we now think of our genes.

There was—and is—nothing necessarily wrong, foolish, or dangerous about studying an aspect of God's creation such as the stars. It all depends what you do with that study. If it leads you to worship Christ, as was the case with the wise men who followed the star to Bethlehem, it can be sensible. If it leads you to worship the stars themselves, then you should stop immediately, since the Bible strictly forbids that practice!

So we need not be frightened by the word *astrology*. We just need to be very clear how we are using it. Like Lewis, we use it here in the pre-Copernican and Christian sense implied by Psalm 19: "The heavens are telling the glory of God."

Lewis didn't literally believe in the medieval planetary influences, but he did think that the planets, because of their traditional associations, were powerful symbols. After all, God had made the planets and so it was only right and proper that they should signify more than just themselves.

Lewis once said, "The characters of the planets, as conceived by medieval astrology, seem to me to have a permanent value as spiritual symbols." When he calls them "spiritual symbols," he means they are useful images or summaries of God's sovereignty, beauty, power, wisdom, and the like. And their usefulness as symbols isn't just for people in earlier times. No, the planets have a *permanent value* as spiritual symbols. That's no small claim.

And Lewis's high view of the heavenly bodies comes through in the Narnia books, where he often makes a special connection between Aslan and the Narnian stars:

- In *The Magician's Nephew*, Aslan says, "I give you the stars and I give you myself."
- In *The Silver Chair*, when the children are lost in the Underworld, they remember the "sun and moon and stars and Aslan himself."
- In *The Last Battle*, Roonwit the Centaur says, "If Aslan were really coming to Narnia . . . all the most gracious stars would be assembled in his honor."

But it is not just the Narnian stars that have a special significance in the Chronicles. I believe Lewis used the symbolism of the seven heavens of *this* world as he wrote the Narnia books. He structured each Chronicle, I think, so that it would embody and express the spiritual quality of one of the seven planets. He kept silent about it, but that is to be expected, since the heavens themselves were believed in medieval times to be constantly singing a music that was effectively silent as far as people on Earth were concerned. Pre-Copernican astronomers called it "the music of the spheres," and Lewis described it as a perpetual *Gloria* eternally exchanged between the angelic spirits who guided the planets in their paths. Paradoxically, it is never heard on Earth because it is *always* heard. We have no negative with which to contrast our positive hearing of this music. It fills our ears every minute of every day and every night.

People who live next door to a railway line don't hear the trains. People who live next to Niagara Falls don't hear the water. And people who lived on Earth before the time of Copernicus didn't hear the music of the spheres. Yet it was always sounding.

Lewis wrote about the music of the spheres in his academic works. He loved the idea of music you are always listening to but can never hear. And when he came to write the Narnia Chronicles, his own version of the music of the spheres sounds on every page of every story.

His favorite planet was Jupiter, and it was out of the spiritual symbolism of Jupiter that he formed the first of the seven Narnia Chronicles, *The Lion, the Witch and the Wardrobe.*

And that will be the subject of our next chapter—by Jove!

CHAPTER FOUR

JUPITER'S KINGLY CROWN

The Lion, the Witch and the Wardrobe

*You shall be a crown of beauty in the hand of the LORD,
and a royal diadem in the hand of your God.*

ISAIAH 62:3

LEWIS WROTE ABOUT the origin of *The Lion, the Witch and the Wardrobe* in private letters and in articles for magazines. Some of his friends and students also recall him speaking about how he came to write his most famous work.

Nowhere in any of these records did Lewis ever mention the planets, let alone Jupiter. So why am I so sure that Jupiter is behind it? Why need *anything* be behind it?

We need not reexamine all the points made in chapters 1 and 2 about how the Narnia books seem a hodgepodge and yet how unlikely it is that Lewis would have written in a slapdash manner. Nor need we mention again his personal capacity for secretiveness, his interest in the *kappa* (or cryptic) element in stories, or that numerous other scholars have gone looking for a hidden theme. Still less need we go over his long-standing love of the planets, which dated at least from the age of ten, when, he said, the planets held a "peculiar, heady attraction" for him.

However, it's worth pointing out two things we haven't so far considered as we listen to what Lewis said about the origin of *The Lion, the Witch and the Wardrobe*. They both help reinforce the possibility of a secret level of meaning.

The first point is that Lewis himself said, quite openly, "You must not believe all that authors tell you about how they wrote their books." They do not mean to tell lies, he added, but they don't always remember the whole process themselves.

And the second point is that, even when authors do remember the whole process, they don't necessarily want to share it with their readers. A famous description of good art is art that hides itself. This line can be found in the ancient Roman poet Ovid: "If art is concealed it succeeds."

Lewis knew and admired Ovid's work, and in many places he himself talked about the importance of indirectness for successful communication. "An influence which cannot evade our consciousness will not go very deep," he once wrote. And in another place he said that an author works best by "powerfully evoking secret associations." He also thought that "what the reader is made to do for himself has a particular importance in literature." A wise writer will not reveal all the cards in his hand, either in the telling of the story or in his comments upon the writing process.

With those things in mind, let's now take a look at what Lewis said about how he came to write *The Lion, the Witch and the Wardrobe*.

"IT ALL BEGAN WITH A PICTURE"

"It all began with a picture." That was how Lewis described the starting point behind *The Lion, the Witch and the Wardrobe*. The whole process "began with a picture of a Faun carrying an umbrella and parcels in a snowy wood." This picture had been in his mind's eye since he was about sixteen years old. One day, many years later, he said to himself, *Let's try to make a story about it.*

At first he wasn't sure how the story would go, and at that early stage, "there wasn't even anything Christian" about the picture in his head. Other pictures gradually presented themselves to his mind. Lewis said the process was a bit like bird-watching: every now and again a new one would fly into view.

These other pictures included "a queen on a sledge" and "a magnificent lion." Slowly they sorted themselves into a sequence of events (in other words, a story). The story was still rather formless—like fruit boiling in a saucepan as you make jam. And then, all of a sudden, "Aslan came bounding into it," and once Aslan arrived, he "pulled the whole story together."

It was obviously important to Lewis that the different parts of the story should be pulled together. This reminds us of the great value he attached to unity and coherence. He wasn't a random or careless writer.

But *how* does Aslan pull the different parts together, and *why* was Lewis so interested in this picture of a faun in a snowy wood carrying an umbrella and parcels?

"WINTER PASSED"

Most people who have studied the way Lewis imagined *The Lion, the Witch and the Wardrobe* are interested only in the part where he says "Aslan came bounding in." People are very interested in this Christlike character (and quite rightly, because he is the most important character), but they don't bother to ask themselves whether anything *connects* the picture of a magnificent lion with the picture of the snowy wood.

Jupiter provides the link. Jupiter, according to Lewis's poem "The

Planets," not only makes people "lion-hearted," he also brings about "winter passed."

The White Witch has made it "always winter." Her kingdom of ice and snow is a curse, a tyranny. This is not a winter wonderland, but the perpetual freeze of death. And almost always in Lewis's works when you come across a mention of winter, you know that Jupiter can't be far behind. It is not just in "The Planets" that you find Jupiter destroying winter. In Lewis's book *The Allegory of Love*, Jupiter brings about "winter overgone." In his novel *That Hideous Strength*, Jupiter comes down to Earth and does away with "freezing wastes" and "unendurable cold." In that same book, the hero, Ransom, who has become a human version of Jupiter himself, defeats enemies with names such as Frost, Wither, Stone, and Winter.

So when Lewis says that he had in his mind a picture of a snowy wood, we ought to be ready for Jupiter to show up and make this wintry landscape summery. Lewis's imagination almost never treats winter as a good thing. It is nearly always a symbol of evils such as fear, punishment, and sorrow.

And the interesting thing is that the picture in his mind's eye actually suggested the evil nature of winter even before Lewis began turning it into a story. The faun is carrying an umbrella. He is trying to *protect* himself from the snow. He is not larking about, throwing snowballs, building snowmen, and letting snowflakes fall on his eyelashes. I thought Walden Media's movie version of the story presented the snowy landscape far too positively. We should feel that the wintry wood is ominous and threatening. There is hardly anything beautiful about it.

When Lewis began to turn this picture into a story, he drew out these meanings of doom and fear. The unnamed faun in the mental picture became, of course, Mr. Tumnus, who is worried about catching cold; the winter makes him gloomy; he has "a melancholy voice." He is anxious to hold the umbrella over Lucy to protect her from the winter too. He is sad because it is "always winter and never Christmas." The parcels that he carries are presumably Christmas parcels—but he won't be able to open them because the White Witch has banned Christmas. If he complains to the Witch about this, he will be turned to stone.

Still, he hasn't given up hope. He longs for the old days of "jollification." *Jollification* is a very important word because jollity and joviality are associated with Jupiter. Gustav Holst's great musical work *The Planets Suite* contains a movement called "Jupiter, the Bringer of Jollity." Lewis knew and loved *The Planets Suite*. He described it as a rich and marvelous work that moved him very greatly.

In *The Lion, the Witch and the Wardobe*, Jupiter's influence brings jollity as winter finally passes and summer comes in. January turns to May. Festivity and revelry replace fear and freezing. Aslan, who sums up the Jovial spirit in his own person, is the means by which this influence makes its presence felt:

> *When he bares his teeth, winter meets its death,*
> *And when he shakes his mane, we shall have spring again.*

THE KING

Aslan is responsible not only for the passing of winter and the coming of jollity. He is also the king. Why? Because Jupiter was the king of the planets, the sovereign of the seven heavens. Kingship, in fact, was Jupiter's main quality, and therefore kingship is central to the plot of *The Lion, the Witch and the Wardrobe*. Is Narnia going to be ruled by Aslan, the King of the wood, or by the Witch, who calls herself empress of Narnia?

Take a look at the first mention of Aslan. First mentions always set the keynote of a story. And at the first mention of Aslan, the children don't know who he is. Of course not: they've never met him! Mr. Beaver tells them "he's the King." And a few moments later, in case they haven't understood, he tells them again that Aslan "is the King of the wood and the son of the great Emperor-beyond-the-Sea. Don't you know who is the King of Beasts?"

Aslan is "the true king," who has a "crown" and a "standard" (a royal flag). He is "royal, solemn," "royal and strong," with a "great, royal head." Interestingly, he is never again, in any of the other Narnia books, described as royal. For some reason, Lewis is keen to emphasize that he is a royal personage in this story. Could it be because he wants to immerse us in Jupiter's symbolism? It would seem possible, given what he wrote in his academic works. In *The Discarded Image*, Lewis observes that the influence of Jupiter "is *Kingly*; but we must think of a King at peace, enthroned, taking his leisure, serene."

And not only is Aslan's kingship emphasized, so is that of the two boys, Peter and Edmund. The story is really a clash of kingship between these brothers. Who is going to be become king of Narnia? Will it be Peter, under Aslan, or will it be Edmund, under the White Witch?

The Witch has ensnared Edmund with her declaration that she wants a boy who will become king of Narnia when she is gone. Soon after that she promises him, "You are to be the Prince and—later on—the King." Edmund is convinced this is his destiny; he wants "to be a Prince (and later a King)"; he thinks "about Turkish Delight and about being a King" and resolves "when I'm King of Narnia" to "make some decent roads"; this "set him off thinking about being a King." Edmund wants to become a king so he can pay Peter back for calling him a beast, but eventually he realizes that "it didn't look now as if the Witch intended to make him a King," and out of nowhere, so it seems, Father Christmas appears, shouting, "Long live the true King!"

The true King is Aslan, and he has his own plans for the four children. Aslan shows Peter "the castle where you are to be King" and the four thrones "in one of which you must sit as King. . . . You will be High King over all the rest." For of course, it turns out that all four children, including Edmund, are crowned at the end of the story, but only after Aslan has demonstrated true kingship in his self-sacrifice for Edmund's sake.

THE CROWN OF THORNS, THE CROWN OF LIFE

And this sacrifice is also, intriguingly, yet *another* feature of Jupiter's character. How so?

Lewis's great friend Charles Williams once wrote a poem that mentioned "Jupiter's red-pierced planet." He was referring to the Great Red Eye or Great Red Spot that astronomers can see on the surface of Jupiter. It's a huge storm, wider than the diameter of Earth. Charles Williams had imagined this Great Red Spot as a bleeding wound.

Lewis commented on this poem and pointed out that "Jupiter, the planet of Kingship, thus wounded" becomes a reflection of "the Divine King wounded on Calvary." Lewis wrote these words the same year that he began seriously to work on *The Lion, the Witch and the Wardrobe*.

Thanks to Williams, Lewis had a specific reason to link Jupiter with Christ's sacrifice on the cross at Calvary. And of course it's this sacrifice that reappears in the opening Narnia book when Aslan dies on the Stone Table, saving Edmund's life and making the prophecy about the four thrones come true.

The grand coronation scene at Cair Paravel is the climax of the story and the high point of the kingly theme. Aslan has suffered and died. Like Jesus, who wore a crown of thorns and was hailed as king of the Jews, Aslan shows his true kingly nature in bleeding and dying for Edmund's sake. As a result, he gains authority even over death and is able to crown all four children and restore true sovereignty to Narnia. When he finally crowns the children, he declares (and the professor later repeats it), "Once a king or queen in Narnia, always a king or queen."

For this reason, it was a great disappointment to me when the film version of *The Lion, the Witch and the Wardrobe* made such a big deal out of the final battle with the Witch—introducing polar bears and rhinoceroses and all sorts of computer-generated imagery—and dealt with the coronation so briefly. The coronation is what the whole story has been leading to:

> In the Great Hall of Cair Paravel—that wonderful hall with
> the ivory roof and the west wall hung with peacock's feathers
> and the eastern door which looks towards the sea, in the
> presence of all their friends and to the sound of trumpets,
> Aslan solemnly crowned them and led them to the four
> thrones amid deafening shouts of "Long Live King Peter!
> Long Live Queen Susan! Long Live King Edmund! Long Live
> Queen Lucy!" . . . So the children sat on their thrones and
> scepters were put into their hands. . . . And that night there
> was a great feast in Cair Paravel, and revelry and dancing,
> and gold flashed and wine flowed.

We can see from Lewis's other works that kingship and jollity and the passing of winter and the sacrifice of Christ on the cross are all linked in his mind through the symbolism of Jupiter. Can we really conclude it's just a coincidence that all these things should also appear together, and so prominently, in this first Narnia tale?

FATHER CHRISTMAS

If you are still inclined to think it's a coincidence, think about Father Christmas. As I pointed out in the first chapter, many critics (including my own younger self!) have complained about Father Christmas appearing in this story. How can characters in Narnia know of Christmas when they show no knowledge of a character called Christ? It looks like a mistake.

In his university lectures Lewis described the Jovial character as "cheerful and festive; those born under Jupiter are apt to be loud-voiced and red-faced." He would then pause and add: "It is obvious under which planet *I* was born!"—which always produced a laugh.

That's because Lewis himself was loud-voiced and red-faced. He looked like a butcher or a prosperous farmer. He had a deep voice and a hearty laugh. Lots of people who have written about him have, interestingly, described him as jovial without realizing the significance the term had for him.

If Lewis was indeed writing his first Narnia Chronicle in order to express Jove's spirit—the Jovial personality—we can see why he was so keen to keep Father Christmas in the story, even though on the face of it Father Christmas doesn't belong there.

Lewis wrote:

> A supreme workman will never break by one note or one
> syllable or one stroke of the brush the living and inward law
> of the work he is producing. But he will break without scruple
> any number of those superficial regularities and orthodoxies
> which little, unimaginative critics mistake for its laws.

Sometimes a storyteller will do what seems illogical on the surface because he knows of a deeper logic going on underneath. If you haven't "grasped the real and inward significance of the work as a whole" then this illogical thing will look like "a mere botch or failure of unity," he said.

Once we see that Jupiter's imagery is the "inward significance" of this story, we will see that Father Christmas is not a "botch."

Quite the contrary. Father Christmas, red-faced, loud-voiced, and jolly is the nearest thing we still have to the Jovial personality in our popular modern culture. That's why Lewis included him in this book. Father Christmas's gladdeningly red cheeks and his bright red robe ("bright as hollyberries") are entirely within the spirit of the work.

HEARING THE SILENT MUSIC OF JUPITER

But *why* would Lewis want to construct *The Lion, the Witch and the Wardrobe* out of the imagery connected with Jupiter? What was the point of it all? If he wanted us to hear the music of Jupiter, why did he not make it obvious?

There are five main reasons, I think.

The first is, simply, his sense of fun, his playfulness. One of Lewis's colleagues and friends, a man named Simon Barrington-Ward, is still alive. I have come to know Simon Barrington-Ward quite well (he's no relation, despite the similarity of our surnames), and when I told him what I had discovered, he replied, "Oh, that would be just like Jack! That's exactly the sort of thing I would expect him to do. He must have roared with laughter as he did that!"

The second reason has already been talked about in chapter 2, where I discussed Lewis's ideas about the *kappa* (or cryptic) element in a story. A good story needs to have an "atmosphere" or a "flavor," and the Jovial spirit running throughout this book provides just that kind of taste or feel.

The third reason has to do with what Lewis himself thought about the importance of keeping the Jovial symbol alive in modern stories. Jupiter is central in the literature of the Middle Ages, and yet he has almost disappeared from the modern imagination. Lewis wanted to make a modern-day home for Jupiter so that his readers could get acquainted with Jupiter's qualities.

The fourth reason is that Lewis wanted to counteract the tendency toward dull and depressing stories. He thought too many of the tales, plays, and poems that people were writing in his day were grim, dark, and meaningless. "Who does not need to be reminded of Jove?" Lewis once asked. We all need to remember the grand, festive, colorful spirit of Jupiter. It is good to tell stories that make people happy!

The fifth and final reason has to do with Lewis's Christian faith. As I mentioned in chapter 2, he thought that we come to know God more by looking *along* the beam than by looking *at* the beam. We need to "breathe the atmosphere" of knowing God. We don't get to know God simply by studying Him from the outside but by recognizing that He is already inside us, holding us and our lives together—indeed, holding the whole universe together.

The children in the story can *look at* Aslan, the kingly lion with his great, royal head, who bleeds to bring about Edmund's rescue. But they need to see that his Jovial spirit is responsible for the rest of the story too. His Jovial spirit does away with the awful winter. His Jovial spirit means there are "royal robes" waiting for them in the Wardrobe. His Jovial spirit allows them to meet Father Christmas. His Jovial spirit enables them to become kings and queens.

Everywhere they look—if only they have eyes to see—they will perceive Aslan's Jovial spirit. All sorts of apparently incidental details—oak trees, thrones, crashing waves on the beach, the peacock feathers on the wall of the castle—are present because they are Jovial symbols and this is, so to speak, a Jovial world. Aslan's Jovial spirit runs through it all—the big things, the medium-sized things, and even the tiniest things, such as the red breast of the robin ("you couldn't have found a robin with a redder chest"). As Lewis commented in one of his academic works, a good writer will pay attention even to "apparent *minutiae*," the minutest aspects of the tale.

THE CASTLE AND THE CROWN

And speaking of details, another little detail worth explaining is the name *Cair Paravel*, which emphasizes again the kingly aspect of Jupiter's personality. *The Lion, the Witch and the Wardrobe* is a tale in which kingliness cascades down from the Emperor-beyond-the-Sea to the King of the wood to the High King Peter, and then to Susan, Edmund, and

Lucy. True sovereign authority submits to the commands of the higher king and results in the service of the lower king, who in turn passes down royalty to the rank below, and so on through all creation.

Cair Paravel helps express this because it is a combination of *cair*, meaning "walled city" or "castle" and *paravail*, meaning "beneath" or "under." A "tenant paravail" holds property under another person who is himself a tenant.

So *Cair Paravel* means something like "castle under castle," which is what we would expect if kingly Jupiter is indeed the inner meaning of the book. In this Jupiter-drenched story, it is no accident that Cair Paravel shines "like a great star resting on the seashore." The Jovial character is everywhere—if we have the eyes to see it.

Lewis turns Jupiter imagery to Christian effect in this, his most famous book. He cleverly uses the planetary symbolism that he had studied so closely in his academic work and about which he had written so much in his poetry and in his earlier fiction. He turns this planet into a plot. He turns this spiritual symbol into a story.

Why? Ultimately, and most importantly, because he believed that Jesus Christ is the "King of kings" (1 Timothy 6:15) and that God will give a "crown of life . . . to those who love him" (James 1:12). Those realities were worth celebrating and telling stories about!

And what Lewis does by means of Jupiter in *The Lion, the Witch and the Wardrobe*, he does with the other six planets in the other six Chronicles.

The next planet to visit is Mars. Forward march!

CHAPTER FIVE

THE WOODEN SHIELD OF MARS

Prince Caspian

Above all, take the shield of faith.
EPHESIANS 6:16

STAR WARS is one of the most famous films ever made. Part of its success is its great soundtrack by John Williams. Williams based it on the Mars movement of *The Planets Suite*, which Gustav Holst composed between 1914 and 1916.

Holst described Mars as "the Bringer of War," and his Mars music is full of threatening drums and blaring brass. It has a pounding beat and is absolutely deafening. It's a brilliant, terrifying piece.

When C. S. Lewis heard *The Planets Suite*, he thought the music for Mars was "brutal and ferocious." He admired what Holst had done, but he also felt there were other aspects of Mars that were worth thinking about, not just the violent side.

LEWIS ON MARS

The name *Lewis* means "famous warrior," and Lewis had—very appropriately—become interested in Mars at an early age. When he was only about six years old, he began to write a short story called "To Mars and Back." When he was forty, he finally finished it! By then it had changed a good deal: it was now a full-length novel called *Out of the Silent Planet*, the first book in his Ransom Trilogy of interplanetary adventures.

The story is set on Mars, which Lewis renames Malacandra. But Lewis doesn't just use Mars for the setting. He uses "Martianity" (as he called it) throughout the whole tale, "emotionally and atmospherically, *as well as* logically."

At the end of the Ransom Trilogy, Mars descends to Earth and makes people martial. One of these people is called Mark, a name meaning "martial, warlike." Mark becomes not "brutal and ferocious" but strong, disciplined, and courageous.

Another character in the story becomes Martial as he remembers the battles he has fought in. He recalls hearing "the *click-click* of steel points in wooden shields."

Wooden shields are key to how Lewis understood the Martial spirit. Shields are obviously connected with Mars because they are weapons, the tools of battle. Less obviously, but no less importantly, they are connected with Mars because they are *wooden*. Mars had a special relationship with the woods. Why? Well, think of the third month of the year.

The third month is called March because Mars made his influence particularly felt at that time of year, according to pre-Copernican astronomers. That is the month when the woods come back to life after winter and regain their leaves.

This explains the two main themes running through *Prince Caspian*. On the one hand, it is a war story. On the other hand, it is a story about woods and forests. Aslan, as we shall see, has a central part to play in both strands of the story.

MARS ON THE MARCH

In *Prince Caspian*, the four Pevensie children find that they have arrived in Narnia "in the middle of a war." It is "the great War of Deliverance," as it is referred to in a later Chronicle, or simply the "Civil War" in Lewis's "Outline of Narnian History." The war is being fought "to drive Miraz out of Narnia" and restore the kingdom to Caspian.

Glenstorm the centaur tells Caspian, "I and my sons are ready for war. When is the battle to be joined?" Caspian had not "really been thinking of a war." Glenstorm tells him, "The time is ripe. I watch the skies. . . . Tarva and Alambil have met in the halls of high heaven."

This refers to the conjunction of two planets—"Tarva, the Lord of Victory," and "Alambil, the Lady of Peace." Caspian has already seen this conjunction with his tutor, Dr. Cornelius, at nighttime from the top of a tower. (These two planets are the first thing moviegoers see in the film version of *Prince Caspian*—an excellent decision on the part of the director.)

In his book on the literature of the sixteenth century, Lewis quotes an author who wrote, "I know by the course of the planettes that there is a Knyght comynge." In *Prince Caspian*, Lewis dramatizes that very thing. Dr. Cornelius tells Caspian that the meeting of these two planets in the night sky "is fortunate and means some great good for the sad realm of Narnia." It is fortunate because it means that Peter, the knight, is coming, who will help bring victory and restore peace to Narnia.

Caspian remembers this planetary conjunction when Glenstorm, a stargazer, reminds him about it. He realizes it is "quite possible that they might win a war and quite certain that they must wage one." He therefore summons a council of war. The council authorizes action, and Caspian leads the skirmishing forces as they engage the army of

Miraz, Caspian's murderous uncle who has wrongly seized the Narnian throne.

Once the Pevensies arrive in Narnia, Peter challenges Miraz to "mono-machy" (single combat). Miraz is killed, not by Peter as it turns out, but by one of his own men, Glozelle, after which full battle is joined.

In addition to these important military events in the story, numerous other episodes are included in *Prince Caspian*: the children's rediscovery of their armor, the rescue of the dwarf from the soldiers, the swordsmanship and archery test, the arrow attack on the children in the wood, the fight with the werewolf and the hag. The cast list consists largely of military figures: armies, warriors, messengers, enemies, captains, sentries, sentinels, knights, and scouts. Caspian's horse, Destrier, has a special connection to Mars because a *destrier* is a warhorse or charger. Queen Prunaprismia's name comes from a Charles Dickens character who is always saying "prunes and prism" and who is called—wait for it!— Mrs. *General*.

All sorts of different armor and weapons are mentioned in the course of the story: mail shirts, helmets, horns, hauberks, daggers, bows, swords, and shields. Attacks, salutes, and sorties are some of the military actions that take place in a variety of military settings: battlements, strongholds, towers, castles, and camps.

These details suggest that Lewis wanted to create a Martial atmosphere, and in fact, the word *martial* appears twice in *Prince Caspian*, the only Chronicle in which it occurs at all. Reepicheep is described as a "martial mouse" and Miraz worries about his "martial policy."

The influence of Mars is suggested also when we hear that some kind of "magic in the air" has possibly saved Susan's bowstring from perishing. As Edmund breathes this atmosphere, he finds that "the air of Narnia" brings "all his old battles . . . back to him." Caspian begins "to harden" as he sleeps "under the stars," receiving the "hard virtue of Mars."

But Caspian doesn't harden into a brutal warrior. He becomes a knight, a particular kind of warrior—disciplined, gallant, self-controlled. Trufflehunter, Trumpkin, and Reepicheep also become knights. In fact, knights appear all over this story! Edmund mentions "knights-errant." In the ruins of Cair Paravel we see "rich suits of armor, like knights guarding the treasures." Edmund is "Knight of the Noble Order of the Table," a "very dangerous knight." Even the chess piece discovered at the start of the story is a chess-knight.

Lewis loved a poem called the *Knight's Tale* by Geoffrey Chaucer (1343–1400) in part, he said, because "the character and influence of the planets are worked into the *Knight's Tale*." Chaucer hadn't just put the planetary characters into his cast list; he had woven their effects into the plot. For example, the climax of the poem happens on a Tuesday to show that Mars is especially at work—Tuesday being Mars's day, as we discussed in chapter 3.

Lewis imitates Chaucer in the way he tells this Narnian story of knighthood. Peter, Knight of the Most Noble Order of the Lion, is the model of true knightly behavior. He is strong enough to defeat the treacherous Sopespian but gentle enough to kiss the furry head of the badger. He has physical courage (risking his body in combat) but also takes care to remember seemingly unimportant traditions, such as the Bears' hereditary right to be marshals (a term that is itself a Martial pun!).

Peter shows true knightly self-control during his single combat with Miraz. When Miraz trips and falls, Peter refuses to attack him while he is down. This annoys Edmund, who is watching from the sidelines. Edmund says: "Oh, bother, bother, bother. Need he be as gentlemanly as all that? I suppose he must. Comes of being a Knight *and* a High King."

Lewis is trying to show us the principles of knightly behavior that he had written about in his academic works. He thought the old ideal of knighthood combined "morality up to the highest self-sacrifice and manners down to the smallest gracefulness in etiquette." Lewis had fought as a soldier in the First World War, but he hated bloodthirstiness. War was sometimes regrettably necessary, he thought, but it should never become an excuse for mindless violence—conducted with a sort of macho, Rambo, slash-and-burn attitude. No, the true warrior should be gentle as well as strong, disciplined as well as fierce.

Military discipline is seen in the way armies move. They don't just walk, and they certainly do not slouch. They march! They move in step to a rhythm with their backs straight and their heads up. This very unnatural way of walking developed for a reason. It helps soldiers feel in their bones the need for physical self-control. It helps prevent the army from becoming a disorderly rabble.

Prince Caspian contains much marching. Peter says, "On the march." Trumpkin says, "I'd as soon march as stand here talking." Aslan's How is "half a day's march" from the Fords of Beruna. Edmund is "Count of the Western March." And this neatly brings us to March in the other sense—the month in springtime when the woods come back to life.

MARS IN THE MONTH OF MARCH

March is the only month named after a planet. And it is interesting that the only Narnian month we ever hear about in any of the Chronicles is "Greenroof"—the month during which all the events of *Prince Caspian* take place.

The reason for the connection with March is that Mars was not always and only associated with war, but was also responsible (under God) for bringing growth and greenness to trees and indeed all kinds of vegetation. In this capacity, Mars was known as Mars Silvanus. The word *silvan* means "related to trees." That is why Lewis puts silvans as well as dryads and hamadryads (different kinds of tree spirit) into *Prince Caspian*. The silvan aspect of Mars also features strongly in

Out of the Silent Planet, so Lewis obviously thought it was an essential component of the Martial influence.

When the children first arrive in Narnia, they land "in a woody place—such a woody place that branches were sticking into them and there was hardly room to move." Peter exclaims, "I can't see a yard in all these trees" for the wood is "thick and tangled," forcing them to "stoop under branches and climb over branches" and blunder "through great masses of stuff like rhododendrons."

Caspian and Dr. Cornelius can't clearly see the conjunction of Tarva and Alambil because a tree is in the way. Caspian comes from a race "who cut down trees wherever they could and were at war with all wild things; and though he himself might be unlike other Telmarines, the trees could not be expected to know this." Trufflehunter regrets that they cannot "wake the spirits of these trees," for "once the Trees moved in anger, our enemies would go mad with fright."

Aslan's How now stands in the middle of the Great Woods, and Caspian's army flees there for safety. Lucy tries to wake the trees in chapter 9, but fails. In chapter 10 the children's progress is hampered by the fir wood, though it provides them with cover when they have to run from the arrows of Miraz's sentries. Later, Lucy finds the trees awake in the presence of Aslan.

The theme reaches its high point when the awakened trees plunge through Peter's army to pursue the Telmarines. The two sides of Mars (the military side and the silvan side) now come together:

> Have you ever stood at the edge of a great wood on a high
> ridge when a wild southwester broke over it in full fury on an
> autumn evening? Imagine that sound. And then imagine that
> the wood, instead of being fixed to one place, was rushing *at*
> you; and was no longer trees but huge people; yet still like trees

because their long arms waved like branches and their heads tossed and leaves fell round them in showers.

Appalled by this onslaught, the Telmarines "flung down their weapons, shrieking, 'The Wood! The Wood! The end of the world!'" They rush to the river, only to find their escape route destroyed: sprouting ivy has pulled down the bridge.

In the final chapter, at night, the trees come forward, throwing off spare strands and fingers, to form a great woodland bonfire. The battle is now over, and Narnia is restored to a "divinely comfortable" state. Tarva, the Lord of Victory, has indeed saluted Alambil, the Lady of Peace.

BACK TO BACCHUS

The war imagery and the woodland imagery show that Lewis deliberately structured *Prince Caspian* so that it would have Mars as its secret inner meaning, its *kappa* element, its unifying atmosphere. But if there is any doubt, we should think about Bacchus.

Bacchus, as I mentioned in chapter 1, always seemed to me—as I know he seemed to many other readers—a strange character to meet in Narnia. Why did he turn up and make everyone merry with wine? What was Lewis playing at?

It becomes clear when we see that Bacchus is another aspect of the Martial theme. In ancient Rome, the Festival of Mars began on the first day of March and lasted for over three weeks. Bacchanalian festivities (ceremonies celebrating Bacchus) were part of that festival, taking place on the sixteenth and seventeenth days of the month.

Lewis puts Bacchus into *Prince Caspian* for the same kind of reason that he put Father Christmas into *The Lion, the Witch and the Wardrobe*. Bacchus is a character who helps personify the planet that provides the secret theme. On the face of things, he doesn't belong; but when you have grasped "the inward significance of the whole work," he makes perfect sense.

HEARING THE SILENT MUSIC OF MARS

The most obvious reason Lewis chose to shape *Prince Caspian* this way is because he thought people needed to be reminded of the Christian ideal of knighthood. In *Mere Christianity* Lewis writes that "the idea of the knight—the Christian in arms for the defence of a good cause—is one of the great Christian ideas."

Lewis lived through two world wars, and he saw how necessary it was to stand up to aggressive dictators, particularly Hitler and the evil of Nazi Germany. And he wasn't the only British person to look to the imagery of Mars when thinking about the war. Winston Churchill, who was prime minister of Great Britain during World War II, once gave a speech in which he said that Nazi power would overrun the whole of Europe unless "by a supreme recovery of moral health and *martial* vigour, we rise again and take our stand for freedom as in the olden times."

It is necessary at times, Lewis thought, to take up arms against evil. Sometimes the weapons are literal weapons—swords and shields—and sometimes they are spiritual. In the Bible, the apostle Paul speaks of the Christian life in terms of soldiering. He encourages Timothy to be "a good soldier of Christ Jesus" (2 Timothy 2:3), and he urges people to "put on the whole armor of God" (Ephesians 6:11).

One particular piece of armor is the shield of faith, and it is interesting that Lewis makes special mention of Peter's shield during the single combat. "Peter's not using his shield properly," says Edmund. That's because Miraz put "the full weight of his shoulder on my shield," Peter explains, "and the rim of the shield drove into my wrist." Edmund helps bind up Peter's wrist, and "the new bout went well" because "Peter now seemed to be able to make some use of his shield."

Lewis never makes it explicit that Peter's shield is the shield of faith, but in one of his academic books he draws special attention to the fact that the "knight of faith" has as his greatest weapon "not his sword but his shield" before quoting the passage in Ephesians 6 where the apostle Paul mentions this spiritual weapon.

Paul once preached in Athens at a place called Mars Hill (Acts 17:19-34). In his sermon, he said God is the one in whom "we live and move and have our being" (Acts 17:28). And this is what Lewis believed too. Because we exist *in* God, we sometimes find it hard to recognize Him. Surrounded and upheld by Him, we often overlook Him!

Lewis was trying to convey this overlookable aspect of God's nature when he structured the Narnia stories out of planetary imagery. The children in *Prince Caspian* don't realize that they exist "in Mars"—Mars used as a symbol for God. They don't understand that the reason they are involved in war is because Mars is in charge. They don't recognize that the reason the trees come alive is because Mars Silvanus is breathing through the woods. They don't realize that all sorts of seemingly random details—like the rediscovered chess-knight—are present because the Knight of all knights is having his day.

However, they can see Aslan, and in Aslan they see this Martial spirit personified. They see Mars incarnated, made flesh. Lewis makes this quite clear, I think, in the way he portrays Aslan in *Prince Caspian*. Aslan is warlike in this story. His great thundering war cry in chapter 11 ("The Lion Roars") signals that the Narnian lord of hosts is at the heart of this war against the powers of darkness:

Aslan, who seemed larger than before, lifted his head, shook his mane, and roared.

The sound, deep and throbbing at first like an organ beginning on a low note, rose and became louder, and then far louder again, till the earth and air were shaking with it. It rose up from that hill and floated across all Narnia. Down in Miraz's

camp men woke, stared palely in one another's faces, and
grasped their weapons. Down below that in the Great River,
now at its coldest hour, the heads and shoulders of the nymphs,
and the great weedy-bearded head of the river-god, rose from
the water. Beyond it, in every field and wood, the alert ears of
rabbits rose from their holes, the sleepy heads of birds came
out from under wings, owls hooted, vixens barked, hedgehogs
grunted, the trees stirred.

This is Aslan's most warlike moment in the story. Interestingly, his roar
not only prepares everyone for battle, it also makes the trees stir.

As well as representing the military side of Mars, then, Aslan represents the woodland side. He can wake the trees—something Lucy had
tried to do but failed because she was on her own. Only when Lucy
is with Aslan do the trees come alive and start moving. Aslan is, so to
speak, the *true* Mars Silvanus. In the Bible, "the trees of the field . . .
clap their hands" for joy when God's will is done (Isaiah 55:12). Lewis
suggests something similar when all the Narnian trees start worshiping Aslan:

> Pale birch-girls were tossing their heads, willow-women pushed
> back their hair from their brooding faces to gaze on Aslan,
> the queenly beeches stood still and adored him, shaggy oak-
> men, lean and melancholy elms, shock-headed hollies (dark
> themselves, but their wives all bright with berries) and gay
> rowans, all bowed and rose again, shouting, "Aslan, Aslan!"
> in their various husky or creaking or wave-like voices.

Just as Aslan embodies the kingly spirit of Jupiter in *The Lion, the Witch
and the Wardrobe*, so he embodies the spirit of Mars in *Prince Caspian*.
He sums up in his own person the spirit that is spread abroad in the rest

of the story—a story of boys hardening into knights and of girls romping in Bacchanalian revelry with the swaying trees and the growing vines.

A DIFFERENT KIND OF TURKISH DELIGHT

The very last words of the story are spoken by Edmund: "Bother!" he says. "I've left my new torch in Narnia."

The electric torch that Edmund was given as a birthday present turns out to be quite important at the start of the adventure. The children can't make sticks burn as torches when they go into the dark treasure chamber of the castle, so they use Edmund's battery torch instead.

Lewis is having a private joke here. He knew some words in Arabic and related languages. The word *aslan*, in fact, is the Turkish for "lion." And the Arabic word for "torch" means not only torch, but also . . . "Mars."

And if that is an accident, my name is Reepicheep!

CHAPTER SIX

SUNLIGHT'S GOLDEN TREASURY

The Voyage of the "Dawn Treader"

Lay up for yourselves treasures in heaven.
MATTHEW 6:20

J. K. ROWLING, the author of the Harry Potter books, has said that she adored the Narnia Chronicles when she was young and rereads them now in adulthood whenever she finds a copy at hand.

If I were trying to spot a connection between J. K. Rowling's stories and C. S. Lewis's, I would point to *Harry Potter and the Philosopher's Stone* (or *Sorcerer's Stone*, as it's called in America).

The philosopher's stone was something scientists tried to find in the Middle Ages and Renaissance. They thought it would allow them to make gold out of base metals—a branch of science called alchemy. They wanted to imitate the influence of the Sun, which was traditionally thought responsible, under God, for making all the gold that already existed in the Earth. This, we might say, was the original understanding of "solar power."

And just as J. K. Rowling puts the philosopher's stone into one of her Harry Potter books, so C. S. Lewis puts the gold-making Sun into one of his Narnia tales, *The Voyage of the "Dawn Treader."*

GOLDFINGER, THE STAR WITH THE MIDAS TOUCH

Lewis was fascinated by the Sun's supposed power to make gold, and he thought it could be used as a symbol of God's ability to save us from our sins, redeeming our base actions and turning them into something much more precious, transforming "the uncomely common to cordial gold," as he put it in "The Planets."

In another of his poems, called "Noon's Intensity," he writes that there will necessarily be "many metals" until the Sun's "alchemic beams" make them all golden.

And in yet another of his poems, called "A Pageant Played in Vain," he imagines himself like the Earth—full of impure soils that need to be purified—and addresses God as if He were the Sun. He prays, "Break, Sun, my crusted earth" and asks that God should penetrate his soul so deeply that "immortal metals" will "have their birth" inside him.

So we see that Lewis had a long-standing interest in alchemy, and when he wrote *The Voyage of the "Dawn Treader,"* he devoted a whole chapter to it. Caspian, Lucy, and the others discover a mysterious pool on an island. They spot a life-size figure of a man at the bottom of the pool:

> It lay face downward with its arms stretched out above its head. And it so happened that as they looked at it, the clouds parted and the sun shone out. The golden shape was lit up from end to end.

The children wonder whether they can pull it out, though Edmund calculates that if it is solid gold, it will be too heavy to lift. When he lowers a spear into the water to test its depth, it becomes so heavy that he has to drop it. Noticing that the tips of his boots have changed color, he sharply orders the others to move back at once.

Edmund explains: "That water turns things into gold. It turned the spear into gold, that's why it got so heavy. And it was just lapping against my feet (it's a good thing I wasn't barefoot) and it turned the toe-caps into gold. And that poor fellow on the bottom—well, you see." The golden statue is the body of one of the seven lost lords they are seeking. In the James Bond movie *Goldfinger*, people are killed by being painted gold. Here in Narnia, death comes through alchemy—through being turned literally golden.

Caspian then dips a spray of heather into the pool. "It was heather that he dipped; what he drew out was a perfect model of heather made of the purest gold, heavy and soft as lead." Immediately, Caspian is overtaken by greed:

> "The King who owned this island," said Caspian slowly, and his
> face flushed as he spoke, "would soon be the richest of all Kings
> of the world. I claim this land forever as a Narnian possession.
> It shall be called Goldwater Island. And I bind all of you to
> secrecy. No one must know of this. Not even Drinian—on pain
> of death, do you hear?"

Edmund bristles when he hears Caspian giving orders, and the two nearly come to blows. Lucy intervenes, calling them "swaggering, bully-ing idiots"—when suddenly she stops, her eyes fixed on a nearby hill. The others quickly see what has captured her attention:

> Across the gray hillside above them—gray, for the heather
> was not yet in bloom—without noise, and without looking

at them, and shining as if he were in bright sunlight though the sun had in fact gone in, passed with slow pace the hugest lion that human eyes have ever seen. In describing the scene Lucy said afterward, "He was the size of an elephant," though at another time she only said, "The size of a cart-horse." But it was not the size that mattered. Nobody dared to ask what it was. They knew it was Aslan.

This is an important passage for three main reasons. First, the final sentences—"Nobody dared to ask what it was. They knew it was Aslan"—are a deliberate echo of the Bible, specifically John 21:12: "None of the disciples dared ask him, 'Who are you?' They knew it was the Lord."

Second, it's important because Aslan appears "shining as if he were in bright sunlight though the sun had in fact gone in." This is a very clear indication that in this book Aslan is being portrayed by means of Sun imagery. He is Solar, just as he was Martial in *Prince Caspian* and Jovial in *The Lion, the Witch and the Wardrobe*.

And the third reason why this episode is so important is that it shows alchemy to be evil. "This is a place with a curse on it," says Reepicheep, and he renames it Deathwater Island. Alchemy is an evil because the desire for worldly riches is overpowering and drives people apart. Only when the children look toward Aslan do they become free of this greed for gold. Aslan's riches bring life, not death. He is the true Sun, "the sun of righteousness," as the Bible puts it (Malachi 4:2). Over the course of the story, the children learn that—as Jesus said in the Gospels—they should "lay up for [themselves] treasures in heaven" (Matthew 6:20) and see all earthly riches in the light of that eternal wealth.

TYRANNOSAURUS, BRONTOSAURUS, DOYOUTHINKHESAWUS

In Greek mythology, the Sun—or the light that comes from the Sun—was represented by the god Apollo. Apollo famously went around killing dragons and lizards. He was known as Apollo Sauroctonus, which means "Apollo the lizard slayer." (See photo of a statue of him on page 152.)

Saura is the Greek word for lizard. A dinosaur is a monstrous lizard. Tolkien may have chosen the name of his chief villain in *The Lord of the Rings*, Sauron, in part because it suggests lizards, dragons, serpents, and worms. *The Voyage of the "Dawn Treader"* includes four such dragon-ish creatures. All of them are killed or defeated as the Sun's influence takes effect.

The first of these defeats occurs on Dragon Island, where we see the death of an old, feeble dragon. This episode is based on a poem called "Hymn to Apollo" by the ancient Greek writer Homer—one of Lewis's all-time favorite authors.

Just before this old dragon dies, Lewis tells us that "the sun beat down." Just after the dragon dies, he says "the sun disappeared." The implication is that the sun has killed the dragon; and even the phrasing of the passage is similar to Homer's "Hymn to Apollo," in which the Greek poet describes the dragon "rent with bitter pangs, . . . drawing great gasps for breath and rolling about that place. An awful noise swelled up unspeakable as she writhed continually this way and that."

However, in *"Dawn Treader,"* it is not Apollo who boasts over the dragon's corpse but Eustace Clarence Scrubb! Eustace "began to feel as if he had fought and killed the dragon instead of merely seeing it die." Eustace thinks he possesses his own kind of Solar power, but his arrogance is soon revealed when he becomes a dragon himself.

Eustace falls asleep on the dead dragon's hoard "with greedy, dragonish thoughts in his heart." When he wakes up, he finds that he is a giant lizard or "serpent with legs." It's a terrible moment for him when he realizes that he is "a monster cut off from the whole human race."

Eustace tries three times to scrape off his dragon skin, but each time he merely uncovers another skin underneath. He begins to despair as he realizes he can't undragon himself; he must lie back and allow Aslan to do it for him: "The very first tear he made was so deep that I thought it had gone right into my heart."

The Sun "hurts and humbles," according to "The Planets." And Aslan has both these effects upon Eustace as he is undragoned: "It hurt worse than anything I've ever felt"; "it hurts like billy-oh"; "and by the way, I'd like to apologize."

As Eustace tells Edmund about his experience, dawn arrives: "Though they could not see the sunrise because of the mountains on their right, they knew it was going on because the sky above them and the bay before them turned the color of roses."

This whole scene is one of the most memorable in any of the Narnia Chronicles, and it prepares the way for the third encounter with a dragon—this one a much briefer adventure when the danger appears in the form of the great Sea Serpent that tries to crush the ship. This time we see how the Sun's influence brings wisdom. (Sol "makes men wise," as Lewis writes in *The Discarded Image*.) Reepicheep, whose normal reaction to anything is to fight it, suddenly acquires a new instinct— a Solar wisdom instead of his usual Martial courage. Reepicheep cries out, "Don't fight! Push!" and as a result the Sea Serpent succeeds only in breaking off the *Dawn Treader*'s carved stern.

That carved stern is shaped like a dragon's tail, the ship's bowsprit is like a dragon's head, and its sides are like dragon wings. The *Dawn Treader* itself is the fourth dragon in the story, and here Lewis shows the power of the lizard-slaying Sun in a new and very interesting way.

The ship is a good ship but not a perfect ship. The *Dawn Treader*, with its dragon shape, is the first ship Caspian has built, and his own cabin is decorated, ominously, with "crimson dragons." Despite his goodness and bravery, Caspian can still be tempted by greed—greed of the most subtle kind.

In the final chapter of the book, we discover that Caspian wants to grab not gold but Aslan's country. He is greedy *for heaven*. So greedy that he is prepared to commit what is effectively suicide. He wants to go over the eastern edge of the world and never be seen in Narnia again.

Caspian is prevented from doing this first by the near mutiny of the ship's company and then by a painful meeting with Aslan: "it was terrible—his eyes." This spiritual crisis brings the lizard-slaying theme to its climax.

Lewis teaches a profound lesson. God's ways are beautiful and desirable—"more to be desired than gold, even much fine gold" (Psalm 19:10). And yet they must not be desired in the wrong way. They cannot be seized. They cannot even be bought. Caspian had hoped he could gain Aslan's country at the price of his own life. But Aslan's country is not for sale!

In the Acts of the Apostles we read about Simon Magus, who offered money to the apostles in the hope that he could share their spiritual power (Acts 8:18-24). Simon Magus gave his name to the sin of *simony*—trying to buy spiritual power or a position within the church.

But God is a God of grace. He gives His gifts freely. And learning this can be a painful lesson. It leaves Caspian white-faced and tearful. Caspian realizes that he can't get to heaven unless Aslan calls him there. At the moment Aslan isn't calling him there; he wants him to go on living in Narnia. Lewis reminds us that God "dwells in unapproachable light" (1 Timothy 6:16) and can only be approached when God desires it once the time is right. And this is not Caspian's time. Aslan makes the dragonish king free from greed—not for gold, but for the very best of things, heaven itself.

This freedom is symbolized in three main ways as the story comes to its close: by the freshening of the sea so that it can be drunk in deep, enriching draughts; by the mysterious current that carries the ship across windless seas; and by the sublime "fate" that directs the last moments of the voyage.

Carried forward by this generous-hearted Solar spirit, the voyagers finally tread the dawn:

> Up came the sun. . . . They could look at the rising sun and see it clearly and see things beyond it. What they saw—eastward, beyond the sun—was a range of mountains. . . . No one in that boat doubted that they were seeing beyond the End of the World into Aslan's country.

But the vision is not the end of the voyage, for there is something even better to experience. The children see "something so white on the green grass that even with their eagles' eyes, they could hardly look at it." (The Sun is "beheld only of eagle's eye," according to Lewis's poem "The Planets.")

What they see is a Lamb. The Lamb invites the children to "come and have breakfast" (a reference to John 21:12, where Jesus says the same to his disciples). And as the Lamb speaks, "his snowy white flushed into tawny gold and his size changed and he was Aslan himself, towering above them and scattering light from his mane."

The final alchemical change of the book comes as the white Lamb is transformed into the golden Lion. His Solar character could hardly be more clearly expressed.

HEARING THE SILENT MUSIC OF SOL

In each of the Chronicles, Lewis imagines the basic plotline and all sorts of incidental details so that they express the planetary influence. And he portrays Aslan in a way that sums up and focuses that influence so that there is a harmony between the Christ character and the world that he has made and the events that he brings about.

The remarkable thing about *The Voyage of the "Dawn Treader"* is how very obvious the Sun imagery is once you notice it. The Solar influence governing the story could be worked out from the very title of the book, because this is a tale about a voyage toward the dawn, the place of the rising sun.

As is the case in the other Chronicles, the planetary influence becomes more intense as the story proceeds, but only in this story is the planet actually located and identified as the destination of the plot: "the very eastern end of the world," "the utter East."

Watching the sunrise on Ramandu's Island is a particularly notable moment: "As Edmund said afterward, 'Though lots of things happened on that trip which *sound* more exciting, that moment was really the most exciting.' For now they knew that they had truly come to the beginning of the End of the World."

Over the course of the voyage, the Sun becomes more and more inescapable: "Every morning when the sun rose out of the sea the curved prow of the *Dawn Treader* stood up right across the middle of the sun. Some thought that the sun looked larger than it looked from Narnia, but others disagreed." Later, "there was no mistaking it." And later still, "The sun when it came up each morning looked twice, if not three times, its usual size."

Since the Sun is so obvious, why did it take more than fifty years for anyone to identify it as the underlying theme of the book? One reason, I believe, is that Lewis's poetry is not very well known: most people don't know of his interest in alchemy and astrology, which he expresses in those poems I quoted at the start of this chapter. Also, people today don't know much about Greek mythology, so we don't connect the slaying of dragons with Apollo, the god of light.

And partly it's because Lewis achieved the very thing he set out to achieve! He puts the reader into an atmosphere we then breathe without noticing. He plays Solar music in every part of the story so that we cannot hear it. He causes us to look along the beam, thereby making the beam invisible to us.

And the really amusing thing is that *The Voyage of the "Dawn Treader"* has not one, but two episodes in which that very thing happens! Twice in the story, characters look along beams of light.

One occasion is when the *Dawn Treader* is trapped in the pitch blackness of the Dark Island. Lucy, who is standing up aloft in the fighting-top, prays a desperate prayer for help. A "tiny speck of light" becomes visible, and "a broad beam of light fell from it upon the ship." We then read, "Lucy looked along the beam and presently saw something in it." Lewis explicitly tells us that Lucy "looked along the beam"—the very phrase he used in "Meditation in a Toolshed," which we discussed in chapter 2. Once she looks along the beam, she no longer sees the beam. Instead, she sees what the beam illuminates—Aslan in the form of an albatross.

Lewis also shows us the difference between looking *along* the beam and looking *at* the beam when Lucy is searching Coriakin's book of spells. Interestingly, "her fingers tingled when she touched it as if it were full of electricity." This is one of those occasions when Lewis uses the word *tingled* with more than one meaning. *Tingle* means "star" in Old English, and Lucy's fingers tingle because Coriakin, the author of this book of spells, is himself a star. The book, therefore, feels charged with his heavenly power.

Lucy is looking for a spell to make hidden things visible. Having found the spell, she utters it, expecting only the monopods to be made visible as a consequence. (The monopods are "duffers"—foolish or unwise people—and the chief duffer's daughter is named Clipsie, which comes from the word *clipsi*, meaning "under eclipse, dark.")

After reciting the spell, Lucy is surprised suddenly to find Aslan with her in the room. She buries her face in his "shining mane" and says it was kind of him to come: "'I have been here all the time,' said he, 'but you have just made me visible.'" Aslan effectively says here what Jesus says in John 8:12: "I am the light of the world."

Lucy's ability to see comes from Aslan, the light of the *"Dawn Treader"* world. She would not have been able to see Coriakin's book, or the room, or the island, or anything at all, if Aslan were not illuminating her whole experience. And just as Aslan enables Lucy to see, so the Solar theme of the book enables *us* to see everything in the story. What we *see* as we read the tale—what we "look at"—is the greed for gold, the slaying of dragons, the treading of the dawn, and many other brilliant adventures. But what we *see by*—what we "look along"—is the Solar symbolism. We read the whole tale inside the beam of the Sun's influence.

INFLUENZA

And in the very final sentence of the story, Lewis makes his point one last time—if we have ears to hear it.

Here we discover that Aunt Alberta thinks Eustace has "become very commonplace and tiresome and it must have been the influence of those Pevensie children." Here, yet again, Lewis is having a private joke—this time with the word *influence*.

In one of his academic works, Lewis had written about the old meaning of *influence*—the effect the planets have upon Earth—warning us to remember that nearly all writers before the time of Copernicus would have used the word *influence* with its planetary meaning in mind. That sense of the word is "glitteringly alive" in "the older writers," Lewis said, but in modern English, as most people speak it, the planetary meaning "is thoroughly dead."

We should realize, therefore, that Aunt Alberta is mistaken. Although she uses the right word, she means the wrong thing by it. The change in Eustace has been caused not by the influence of the Pevensie children, but by the *influenza* of the Sun!

CHAPTER SEVEN

MIRROR OR MOONSHINE?

The Silver Chair

The moon will shine like the sun . . . when the LORD binds up the bruises of his people.

ISAIAH 30:26

IN THE BIBLE we read these intriguing words:

The sun will not harm you by day,
*   nor the moon by night.*   PSALM 121:6, NIV

It's obvious how the Sun can harm us: it can cause sunburn and skin cancer; it can leave us dehydrated.

But how can the Moon harm us?

Here is where we need to remember the old view of the heavens—the pre-Copernican view.

Because the Moon changes shape and size so quickly and moves about the night sky so rapidly, sometimes disappearing altogether, it became a symbol of madness. A mentally unstable person—someone who was always changing, never the same—was thought to be under the influence of the Moon, or "Luna," to use another of the Moon's names. In short, he or she was a *lunatic*.

Jesus healed "lunatics" on at least two occasions, according to the Gospel of Matthew (Matthew 4:24; 17:15, kjv). Modern translations of the Bible usually translate *lunatic* as "epileptic." But this is misleading. A friend of mine suffers from epilepsy, and he is certainly not crazy!

If you look at the original Greek word Matthew used, you see that the people Jesus healed were "Selenites," or "those who had been Selenized"—they were under the influence of Selene, who was believed to be a goddess of the Moon. That was how the Moon could hurt you by night. You could go crazy—stark-raving bonkers!

When C. S. Lewis wrote *The Silver Chair*, he constructed the story out of Moon imagery, which is why the tale contains not one but two lunatics. One of them is the headmistress of Jill and Eustace's school, Experiment House, and the way Lewis writes about her is very funny. At the end of the story, the headmistress is found "behaving like a lunatic"—she has hysterics and phones the police with tales about a lion escaped from the circus and escaped prisoners who broke down walls and carried swords:

> After that, the Head's friends saw that the Head was no use
> as a Head, so they got her made an Inspector to interfere with
> other Heads. And when they found she wasn't much good even
> at that, they got her into Parliament where she lived happily
> ever after.

But the other lunatic in *The Silver Chair* is much more serious. This is the lost Prince Rilian, who says:

Every night there comes an hour when my mind is most
horribly changed. . . . I become furious and wild and would
rush upon my dearest friends to kill them, if I were not bound.
. . . I myself know nothing of it, for when my hour is past I
awake forgetful of all that vile fit and in my proper shape and
sound mind.

As it happens, Prince Rilian is not telling the truth. His hour of madness is actually his only moment of sanity. The fact that he lies about
this (without even knowing he is lying) is part of his lunacy. It leaves Jill,
Eustace, and Puddleglum totally confused.

When Rilian begs them in Aslan's name to free him from his bonds,
they don't know what to do. "Could Aslan have really meant them to
unbind anyone—even a lunatic—who asked it in his name?"

We will return to Prince Rilian later, but first let's explore further why
the Moon was connected to madness. We've already noted the Moon's
changeableness. There were two other symbolic links to lunacy: one has
to do with water and one with "moonshine."

WET, WET, WET

If you look at what Lewis wrote about the Moon in his poem "The
Planets," you will see how strongly it was associated with water. The
poem mentions dew and drenching and drizzling, showers and moisture.
The link between the Moon and wetness came about because of the
Moon's influence upon Earth's tides. Our seas and rivers are affected by
the Moon's gravitational pull.

Lewis has the Moon's drenching, drizzling, dewy effects in mind
throughout *The Silver Chair*. The theme is introduced at the very start
of the story, when we first meet Jill Pole, who is crying on a "damp
little path." Eustace joins her, sitting down on "grass [that] was soaking wet." Lewis also describes drops that "dripped off the laurel leaves,"

that "drip off the leaves," and of "drops of water on the grass." These images, seemingly irrelevant to the plot, are there to help create a definite atmosphere.

In the second chapter, water has a more obvious role to play, as seen in Jill's tears and the stream from which she is desperate to drink. After she has quenched her thirst, Aslan blows her down from his high country above the clouds into Narnia, and in his breath she can move as freely "as you can in water (if you've learned to float really well)." She is blown into the "wet fogginess" of a cloud and emerges with wet clothes; she is then splashed by a wave of the sea "drenching her nearly to the waist." She exclaims at the very end of the chapter, "How wet I am!"

We needn't go through every other reference to water and wetness in the book, but others include Jill's baths in chapters 3 and 8, her wet pillow, the frequent rain (mentioned at least six times), Caspian's "watery" eyes, the fountain where Rilian's mother was killed, the marshes in chapter 5 with their "muddy water" and their "countless channels of water," and above all the Marsh-wiggle Puddleglum.

Not only does Puddleglum's name indicate his link with the Moon, but he also does "watery" work and is three times described as a "wet blanket." He imagines that Jill and Eustace have come to him because there's been a flood, he says his firewood may be wet, his pipe smoke trickles out of his bowl like "mist," he mentions the river Shribble and its lack of bridges, predicts "damp bowstrings," snores like a waterfall, and wonders if rain is on its way.

Puddleglum leads Jill and Eustace on their quest. They ford the Shribble (which makes Jill wet to the knees), pass "countless streams" on Ettinsmoor, and are "never short of water." They spot a river "full of rapids and waterfalls" and become "sick of wind and rain." On their way to Harfang, they endure "nasty wet business" and everyone gets wet, "too wet by now to bother about being a bit wetter." The gnomes of Bism row them in a boat on an underground sea; Rilian's words are "like cold water down the back," but later they are glad to find real "water for washing."

Eventually a flood does indeed come to destroy things, as Puddleglum had feared at the start, but it is the Witch's kingdom, not Narnia, that is drowned. Even at the end of the story Puddleglum is still continuing to point out that "bright mornings" bring on "wet afternoons."

The wetness of the Moon's influence is everywhere in this story, and it helps reinforce the idea that things are constantly at risk of sinking into lunacy. Water, by definition, isn't solid; it's liquid. It moves, it changes, it's unsupportive. In that respect it's like the unstable mind of a lunatic.

There's an ever-present danger in *The Silver Chair* that things are going to tip over from sanity into madness. "Lady Luna, in light canoe" is how Lewis writes about the Moon in "The Planets." Think of how a canoeist capsizes and so is suspended head down in the water until he is able to right himself. Becoming permanently capsized is the terrifying prospect facing everyone in this story.

BY THE LIGHT OF THE SILVERY MOON

Another way in which this danger is conveyed is through the imagery of the Moon's silvery light. In the pre-Copernican model of the heavens, the Moon was responsible for making silver on Earth, just as the Sun was responsible for gold.

The most obvious silver thing in the book is the chair of the title—though there are many other objects, such as Trumpkin's "silver ear-trumpet," Rilian's "silver mail," and the lamp in Jill's castle room that hangs by "a silver chain."

The silver chair, where Rilian is tied every night for an hour, is a clear symbol of madness. Why so? Given that Rilian's only time of sanity is the hour when he is tied to the chair, how does the chair symbolize lunacy?

It suggests lunacy because Rilian is *bound* to the chair. He is not free. The one hour in the day when he ought to be able to escape to Overland, he is unable to do so. It's as though a canoeist had to stay head down in the river all the time. It's not crazy to capsize, but it is crazy to stay capsized.

Rilian says, "Let me out, let me go back. Let me feel the wind and see the sky. . . . There used to be a little pool. When you looked down into it you could see all the trees growing upside-down in the water, all green, and below them, deep, very deep, the blue sky."

Rilian's mind is the wrong way up. The highest metal he knows is silver, when in fact silver is not the highest or best metal; the highest is gold. But there is no real gold in his world, just the Witch with her "silver laughs."

The Witch won't allow Rilian to think about gold or the sun. When she takes him up to travel in Overland, he has to wear a heavy black suit of armor, with his visor down. And when they are in Underland, the Witch denies that the golden sun even exists.

"What is this *sun* that you all speak of? Do you mean anything by the word?" the Witch asks.

Rilian replies, "You see that lamp. It is round and yellow and gives light to the whole room; and hangeth moreover from the roof. Now that thing which we call the sun is like the lamp, only far greater and brighter. It giveth light to the whole Overworld and hangeth in the sky."

"Hangeth from what, my lord?" asks the Witch, and while Eustace, Jill, Puddleglum, and Rilian are all still thinking how to answer, she adds, with a soft, silvery laugh, "You see? When you try to think out clearly what this *sun* must be, you cannot tell me. You can only tell me it is like the lamp. Your *sun* is a dream; and there is nothing in that dream that was not copied from the lamp. The lamp is the real thing; the *sun* is but a tale, a children's story."

This is the very definition of lunacy. The Witch is determined to pretend that her silver kingdom is the highest reality. She wishes there to be no sunlight, but only moonlight—which is madness because the Moon can only shine if the Sun first shines upon it. The Moon has no light of its own. As Lewis wrote in another place, moonlight "is only sunlight at second hand."

In one of his earliest poems, Lewis wrote that the Moon is "a stone that catches the sun's beam." And throughout his works he uses the term *moonshine* to mean "nonsense, stupidity." To think that the moon shines with its own light is ridiculous. Yet this is what the Witch wishes to make Rilian and his rescuers believe.

The Witch is also known as the Lady of the Green Kirtle. She is actually a snake, the snake "green as poison" that killed Rilian's mother. And her green attire adds another little touch of Lunar imagery. Shakespeare writes in *Romeo and Juliet* of the clothes "sick and green" that are worn by "the envious Moon." Green is the color of envy, and here Lewis suggests that lunacy is the result of the Moon's being envious of the Sun.

Lewis explicitly refers to another of Shakespeare's plays, *Hamlet*, when he writes that Prince Rilian is "dressed in black and altogether looked a little bit like Hamlet." In his academic writings, Lewis refers to Hamlet as a lunatic, a man "with his mind on the frontier of two worlds . . . unable quite to reject or quite to admit the supernatural." And this idea of the frontier is another important aspect of Lunar symbolism.

In pre-Copernican astronomy, the Moon marked a major frontier. Above the Moon, everything was believed to be perfect, certain, and permanent. Below the Moon, everything was thought to be subject to doubt, confusion, and change. And it's because the Moon stood at the boundary between those two worlds that Lewis structured *The Silver Chair* the way he did.

The difference between Aslan's country and Narnia is clearly modeled on this divide. We read of "the freshness of the air" in Aslan's country, which leads Jill to believe "they must be on the top of a very high mountain" even though "there was not a breath of wind." As they look down, Jill and Eustace see little white shapes far beneath them. At first they appear to be sheep, but they are actually clouds.

Aslan gives Jill four signs to help her and Eustace find Prince Rilian. He then gives her a warning: "Here on the mountain, the air is clear and your mind is clear; as you drop down into Narnia, the air will thicken. Take great care that it does not confuse your mind. And the signs which you have learned here will not look at all as you expect them to look, when you meet them there."

In fact, Eustace does not realize that the old man he sees departing on a ship is the same Caspian whom he had known as a young king. The adventurers do not perceive that the trenches they fall into are really huge letters carved in the rock.

Ignorance, forgetfulness, rain, wind, and snow all help befuddle the travelers' minds, and Jill gives up repeating the signs to herself. The confusion continues until, in chapter 10 ("Travels Without the Sun"), their situation gets even worse. They descend into a yet *more* confusing world when they fall down into Underland, having built a barrier between themselves and Narnia.

In Underland Jill feels she is being "smothered"; the place is "suffocating"; they begin to wonder whether "sun and blue skies and wind and birds had not been only a dream." As she, Eustace, and Puddleglum are repeatedly told, "Many fall down, and few return to the sunlit lands."

Sunlessness, madness, silver, envy, wetness, and wanderings dominate this Lunar tale. One final touch Lewis includes to suggest the Moon's influence is in the names of the two horses that the prince, Puddleglum, Eustace, and Jill ride once the Witch is dead. They are based on the two horses, one pitch black and the other pure white, that in mythology drew the Moon's chariot across the heavens. Lewis calls them Coalblack and Snowflake.

HEARING THE SILENT MUSIC OF LUNA

This is all very interesting, you may say, but what's the point? Didn't Lewis say that the Narnia books were about Christ? What does all this Moon imagery have to do with Christ?

The message Lewis conveys in *The Silver Chair* can be summed up in Jesus' words: "Seek first the kingdom of God" (Matthew 6:33, NKJV). In other words, put first things first. Do not think that this world, the Earth, is eternal. As the apostle Paul writes in Colossians 3:2, "Set your minds on things above, not on earthly things" (NIV).

Aslan doesn't appear bodily in Narnia in this story. Apart from one brief appearance in Jill's dream, Aslan is confined to his own high country above the clouds. The children encounter him in person only before they enter Narnia and after they leave it.

And what Aslan says at the start of the book is absolutely central to Lewis's Christian purpose in this story. Aslan tells Jill:

Remember, remember, remember the signs. Say them to yourself when you wake in the morning and when you lie down at night, and when you wake in the middle of the night. And whatever strange things may happen to you, let nothing turn your mind from following the signs.

This is similar to God's advice to the people of Israel in the Old Testament: "And these words which I command you this day shall be upon your heart; and you shall teach them diligently to your children, and shall talk of them when you sit in your house, and when you walk by the way, and when you lie down, and when you rise" (Deuteronomy 6:6-7).

In some ways the children and Puddleglum fail to learn this difficult lesson. For example, they can't resist thinking about the warm baths and the tasty hot meals the Witch promises will await them at Harfang. As a result they temporarily forget the signs and almost get eaten by giants!

They come very close to failing again once they are in the Under-world. The Witch argues that the supposed supernatural realities—what she calls "fancies" (a term Lewis often used when writing about the Moon)—are taken from Underworld images (sun from lamp, lion from cat) and that the higher world of Narnia does not really exist: "You can put nothing into your make-believe without copying it from the real world, this world of mine, which is the only world."

Rilian, who had earlier won freedom for himself by recalling "the bright skies of Overland . . . the great Lion . . . Aslan himself," is now overpowered again by the lulling words of the Witch, the soft thrumming of her music, and the sweet smell from her fire.

Eustace struggles to recall "the sky and the sun and the stars." But he, too, is soon overpowered, declaring there "never was such a world."

Then Puddleglum remembers the heavens: "I've seen the sun coming up out of the sea of a morning and sinking behind the mountains at night. And I've seen him up in the midday sky when I couldn't look at him for brightness."

"What is this *sun* that you all speak of?" asks the Witch. "There never was a *sun*."

"No. There never was a sun," said the prince, Puddleglum, and the children.

However, Lewis's message is not simply that the Witch is wrong and the rescuers are right. He wants to show how they finally manage to clear their heads. The Witch's "false, mocking fancy" (as Lewis describes the Moon in his early poem "French Nocturne") is extremely convincing. How can they possibly avoid ending up as lunatics?

Only obedience can do it. Painful obedience. Puddleglum stamps on the fire. "He knew it would hurt him badly enough; and so it did." But "the pain itself made Puddleglum's head for a moment perfectly clear and he knew exactly what he really thought. There is nothing like a good shock of pain for dissolving certain kinds of magic."

By reaching for his memory of Overworld through an excruciating act of self-denial, the heroic Marsh-wiggle avoids becoming a lunatic. He ends up limping with the pain, but that is better than submitting to the Witch. As Jesus says in the Gospels, "It is better for you to lose one part of your body than for your whole body to be thrown into hell" (Matthew 5:29, NIV).

As a result of Puddleglum's bravery, order is restored: first things are put first and second things second. In the final chapter, "The Healing of Harms," Jill and Eustace find themselves again in "a great brightness of mid-summer sunshine" in Aslan's high country above the clouds. It reminds us of the description of his country at the start of the story where Jill and Eustace see a "blaze of sunshine" that pours upon them as "the light of a June day pours into a garage when you open the door."

Lewis once wrote that, in relation to God, we should be like "a mirror filled with light," or like "a body ever more completely uncovered to the meridian blaze of the spiritual sun."

The question *The Silver Chair* asks of us is this: will we reflect God's light in our lives or make ourselves out to be suns of our own creating?

Mirrors? Or moonshine?

CHAPTER EIGHT

MERCURY'S WINGED CAP

The Horse and His Boy

The word of God is living and active.

HEBREWS 4:12

IMAGINE YOU LIVED IN the days before electricity. You have no television, no telephone. There are no electric streetlights outside your house.

Night falls, and you can actually see the planets and stars because there's no light pollution. You're not distracted by having to watch the latest DVD—because you have no DVD player. DVDs have not been invented. So what do you watch instead?

You sit outside your house, and you look up at the heavenly bodies in the night sky. Night after night you do this. Year after year.

You notice one particularly small and fast-moving planet. It pops up above the horizon briefly before sunrise. It chases the Sun over the horizon at dusk. *Why does it act like that?* you ask yourself. You have plenty of time to wonder about such questions because you're not wasting hours of each day on Facebook. You have no Facebook. The Internet doesn't exist.

Perhaps that little planet is a young planet, lively and energetic—jumping up and running away again like a child playing outside the window. Perhaps it keeps close to the Sun because it's a messenger, carrying notes from the Sun to the other planets. Perhaps it's also conducting business, buying and selling things, as it shuttles back and forth.

These are the stories you begin to tell to yourself, based on what you can see of Mercury. And your neighbors tell similar stories. Everyone you know has been pondering the significance of the heavens for as long as you've known them. That's what people do. It's what people have *always* done.

This must have been what it was like to live in the olden days, before electricity, before the telescope, before Copernicus. It's no wonder each planet gradually acquired a whole host of meanings and myths associated with it.

In Mercury's case, the planet was deemed "the messenger" and therefore good with words. Mercury was responsible for business. Our word *commerce* means "connected with Mercury." He became linked with anything that went to and fro or that came together only to be separated again. He was associated with things as various as theft and boxing and even had a special connection with crossroads!

C. S. Lewis loved "that shining suburb of the Sun," as he called Mercury in one of his poems. But he found it hard to sum up all of Mercury's different qualities. Rather than trying to define it in words, he suggested looking at Mercury's metal, which is—not surprisingly—mercury (also known as quicksilver).

"Take some real mercury in a saucer and play with it for a few minutes," Lewis advises. "*That* is what 'Mercurial' means." No one today recommends casually playing with mercury because it is not a very safe thing to do. Still, if you want to understand what Mercury symbolizes, just think of quicksilver—the way it rolls about in glittering drops, rapidly splitting and recombining, a metal that is partly liquid and partly solid.

Mercury is listed in the periodic table of elements as Hg, which stands for *hydrargyrum*, a word made up of "hydra" (water) and "argent" (silver). Mercury is literally silver-water or watery silver.

Lewis so loved quicksilver that he inserted a reference to it in *The Horse and His Boy*. In chapter 9, "Across the Desert," we read, "Under the moonlight the sand, in every direction and as far as they could see, gleamed as if it were smooth water or a great silver tray."

Lewis cannot tilt this silver tray of water, as he suggests doing to a saucer of brilliant quicksilver, in order to make its contents divide and roll about in sparkling globules. However, he does show us what happens to it when dawn arrives: "Suddenly the sun rose and everything changed in a moment. The grey sand turned yellow and twinkled as if it were strewn with diamonds."

That is what "Mercurial" means!

THE TWINS

In Lewis's poem "The Planets," Mercury brings about "meeting selves, same but sundered." This is a very important phrase for helping us understand why he wrote *The Horse and His Boy* the way he did.

The Horse and His Boy is a story about twin brothers, Cor and Corin, who were separated shortly after birth and are reunited many years later. They are identical. They were parted. They come back together again. "Meeting selves, same but sundered." Cor and Corin are like drops of mercury.

In Lewis's novel *That Hideous Strength*, a couple of characters meet each other "like two drops of quicksilver." Here in *The Horse and His*

Boy, Lewis doesn't *tell* us that the twin brothers are like drops of mercury, but he shapes the whole story out of Mercurial imagery so we feel it from the inside.

And in fact Cor and Corin are not just any old twin brothers; they are based on a very special pair of twins named Castor and Pollux, characters in one of the greatest of all classical poems, *The Iliad* by Homer. These twins were so famous in ancient times that they are even mentioned in the Bible. In Acts 28:11, the apostle Paul mentions travelling in a ship that has "the Twin Brothers" for its figurehead. This "twin-born progeny," Castor and Pollux, also appear in one of Lewis's poems.

In *The Iliad* Homer describes Castor as a great breaker of horses and Pollux as a mighty boxer. Cor—who is known as Shasta for most of the story—is based on Castor. That's why Lewis gave him those two names: Cor/Shasta = Castor. Shasta becomes a great breaker of horses over the course of this story.

Shasta doesn't "break" Bree in the literal sense of taming him: Bree is already a great warhorse. Nevertheless, Shasta is a "horse-boy" who acquires "a true horseman's seat" and who breaks Bree's pride and self-conceit. Bree admits, "At least [Shasta] ran in the right direction: ran *back*. And that is what shames me most of all. I, who called myself a war horse and boasted of a hundred fights, to be beaten by a little human boy—a child, a mere foal."

And just as Shasta is based on Castor, so Corin is based on Pollux. Corin is a great fighter: he wants to "box" Rabadash; no one "could ever equal Corin as a boxer"; and after he has "boxed" the lapsed bear of Stormness "without a time-keeper for thirty-three rounds," he gains the nickname "Corin Thunder-Fist." According to mythology, Hermes (the Greek equivalent of the Roman Mercury) invented boxing.

And what do Castor and Pollux have to do with Mercury? In myth, the two brothers were turned into stars after they died and so became the constellation Gemini (the Twins). And Gemini is one of the constellations that Mercury "ruled."

This helps explain the other pairs of brothers (Dar and Darrin, Cole and Colin) who appear in the story. Their presence also signifies the Mercurial twinning influence.

QUICKSILVER

And it is not just twin brothers who are brought together like drops of mercury. Shasta is united with Bree; Aravis is united with Hwin; roaring lions then drive these pairs close to each other. At one point Bree veers off to the right just as Hwin veers off to the left, but they are then forced back together "neck to neck and knee to knee," "side by side."

In Tashbaan they separate (Shasta with the Narnians, Aravis with Lasaraleen, the horses with the stable-hand) but are reunited at the Tombs before journeying together across the desert. At the Hermit's house, Shasta runs on ahead, alone, but returns there later.

The separating and uniting imagery is summed up very amusingly near the end of the book, when we're told that Shasta and Aravis have become "so used to quarrelling and making up again that they got married so as to go on doing it more conveniently."

Mercury was the god of the crossroads, and in ancient Greece statues of him were set up as boundary markers or signposts at important junctions. This helps explain why the story so often mentions the taking of different directions. Inside Tashbaan, "everyone seemed to be going either to the left or right." Aravis and Lasaraleen have to go "either left or right." Shasta, in the mountain pass, finds that "the road divided into two" and realizes that "if I stay at the crossroads I'm *sure* to be caught."

Speed is of Mercury's essence, and there is a great sense of urgency throughout the tale. The cry "Narnia and the North!" is heard repeatedly. Bree gallops for sheer joy, then for sheer terror. Aravis says,

"There's not a moment to lose" after overhearing Rabadash's plans. Aslan chases them to the Hermit's dwelling, causing Bree to discover that he has "not really been going as fast—not quite as fast—as he could." Aravis mentions "swift horses"; Rabadash refers to the "swift-est of the galleys"; the Tisroc urges his son to "be swift"; a river is "far too swift" for swimming; Aslan is "swift of foot"; Chervy has "speed"; Shasta is told to "run now, without a moment's rest . . . run, run: always run"; he sees a slope of grass and "a little heather running up before him . . . he had only to run."

Chapter 9 ends with the word "slowly," signaling that something is going dangerously wrong. When I read *The Horse and His Boy* as a child, I disliked this long journey across the desert that seemed to get slower and slower. I now realize that I was *meant* to dislike it!

One way Lewis tries to get us to feel the character of the planet in each Chronicle is by showing us the *opposite* of its influence. The un-Jovial winter is there in *The Lion, the Witch and the Wardrobe* so that we will long for Jupiter's summery spirit to make itself felt. The un-Martial Telmarines in *Prince Caspian* (those undisciplined dandies) are there to show us how much better the Martial armies of Aslan are. Bree's lazy idling in *The Horse and His Boy* helps us feel how vital it is to be quick in this tale.

Of course, Mercury was swift not for the sake of swiftness but because he was "the messenger." When Shasta sprints off with his message for the King of Archenland, Lewis wants us to think of the traditional picture of Mercury with wings on his heels. (See photo on page 154.)

And in case we are in any doubt about the Mercurial theme of the book, Lewis makes it unmistakable in chapter 4, when Shasta sees a Narnian lord wearing a special hat. It is a steel or silver cap "with little wings on each side." This is an obvious reference to Mercury's winged headgear. It was called the "*Petasus*, or Mercurial hat," according to Lewis in one of his academic books.

Pauline Baynes, who illustrated the Narnia books, drew a picture for the first edition of *The Horse and His Boy* showing this winged cap but never knew why Lewis included it. Before she died in 2009, I wrote and asked her, and she said he never told her anything about the planets. In fact, he didn't tell her what to draw at all. In another letter, this one to Lewis scholar Walter Hooper, Baynes said, "I had rather the feeling that, having got the story written down and out of his mind, that the rest was someone else's job, and that he wouldn't interfere."

Lewis's silence on this point is ironic since Mercury was believed to make people skilled in speech. This is why, in America, there are Mercury cell phones and why in Britain the main telecommunications company has an image of Mercury as its corporate logo. In "The Planets," Lewis calls Mercury the "lord of language." And this aspect is very much at the fore in *The Horse and His Boy*, as we will now see.

THE LORD OF LANGUAGE

From the very start of the story we learn how *un*-Mercurial the Calormenes are in the way they speak. The Calormenes liked "talking to one another very slowly about things that sounded dull." We are told of their "loquacity" and "idle words." We hear their vain repetitions about the Tisroc ("may he live forever") and are informed by Bree that this is "slaves' and fools' talk," "Southern jargon."

Here are some examples of Calormene proverbs:

Application to business is the root of prosperity, but those who ask questions that do not concern them are steering the ship of folly toward the rock of indigence.

As a costly jewel retains its value even if hidden in a dung-hill, so old age and discretion are to be respected even in the vile persons of our subjects.

Nothing is more suitable to persons of gravity and decorum than to endure minor inconveniences with constancy.

In contrast, Narnian proverbs are brief, pithy, and witty:

Easily in but not easily out, as the lobster said in the lobster pot!

Maybe Apes will grow honest.

Come, live with me and you'll know me.

Nests before eggs.

At the end of the story Shasta and Aravis attend the grand feast at Anvard. They expect to be bored as the bard and his fiddlers step forward, "for the only poetry they knew was the Calormene kind, and you know now what that was like. But at the very first scrape of the fiddles a rocket seemed to go up inside their heads."

Rocket is a word that Lewis likes to use in connection with Mercury. For instance, when Mercury descends to Earth in *That Hideous Strength*, he sets off "skyrockets of metaphor and allusion" in people's minds, and Lewis uses the word again in relation to Mercury in his book on sixteenth-century literature.

In *The Horse and His Boy*, the theme of language can also be seen in the way Lewis presents the two horses. Both Bree and Hwin pretended, while living in Calormen, not to be talking animals. Early on, Shasta says to Bree, "I wish *you* could talk, old fellow." Bree reveals that he can indeed speak but that, ever since he was taken captive by the Calormenes, he has been pretending to be "dumb and witless like *their* horses." As the story progresses and they escape to Narnia, Mercury (that is, Aslan-as-Mercury) frees them from that silent state.

HEARING THE SILENT MUSIC OF MERCURY

When we ask why Lewis chose to structure *The Horse and His Boy* out of Mercurial imagery, the most obvious factor to consider is the depiction of Aslan. The first time Aslan speaks in this story is when he meets Shasta in the mountain pass. It is night, and Shasta doesn't know who it is who is talking with him in the darkness.

Shasta asks his unwelcome fellow traveler, "Don't you think it was bad luck to meet so many lions?" Aslan replies, "There was only one lion." Shasta is confused: "What on earth do you mean? I've just told you there were at least two the first night, and—"

He is interrupted: "There was only one; but he was swift of foot." "How do you know?" asks Shasta.

> "I was the lion." And as Shasta gaped with open mouth and said nothing, the Voice continued. "I was the lion who forced you to join with Aravis. I was the cat who comforted you among the houses of the dead. I was the lion who drove the jackals from you while you slept. I was the lion who gave the Horses the new strength of fear for the last mile so that you should reach King Lune in time. And I was the lion you do not remember who pushed the boat in which you lay, a child near death, so that it came to shore where a man sat, wakeful at midnight, to receive you."

Aslan sums up—or we might say he incarnates—the spirit of Mercury in his own person. Aslan is "swift of foot"—much swifter than anyone else in this story. Shasta had thought there were several lions, but it turns out they were all one lion. In America the national motto is *e pluribus unum*—"out of many, one." The fifty states make up one Union: the United States of America. The United Kingdom is made up of the four nations of England, Northern Ireland, Scotland, and Wales. The many lions and cats in *The Horse and His Boy* make up one Aslan. Again, this is an example of Mercury's qualities, that "merry multitude of meeting selves," as Lewis puts it in "The Planets."

But Mercury's influence works both ways. Sometimes he makes one out of many. At other times he makes many out of one. And this helps explain the following exchange between Shasta and Aslan:

> "Who *are* you?" asked Shasta.
>
> "Myself," said the Voice, very deep and low so that the earth shook: and again "Myself," loud and clear and gay: and then the third time "Myself," whispered so softly you could hardly hear it, and yet it seemed to come from all round you as if the leaves rustled with it.

In this passage, Lewis very cleverly uses the Mercurial imagery to suggest that Aslan has three aspects. He is reminding us that God is one God in three persons—Father, Son, and Holy Spirit.

In mythology, the Greek version of Mercury was sometimes called Hermes Trismegistus, which means "Thrice-Great Hermes," or "three times great Hermes." Christians in the Middle Ages, looking back at the classical past, thought that the ancient Greeks had been given a glimpse of the Trinity. This "thrice-great" version of Mercury was—so some people thought—a rough impression of the true God. Jesus Christ taught His disciples to baptize people "in the name of the Father and of the Son and of the Holy Spirit" (Matthew 28:19). Three persons but *one* God.

As well as allowing Lewis to say something about the Holy Trinity, the imagery of Mercury also allowed him to say something about "the divine Word."

"In the beginning was the Word," says John at the start of his Gospel (John 1:1). The Word is a title for God, and it is interesting to note that Aslan is not referred to as "Aslan" during his encounter with Shasta in the mountain pass. He is called "the Large Voice," and finally just "the Voice."

Shasta, in contrast, has barely any voice at all: "'Who are you?' he said, scarcely above a whisper." In reply, Aslan utters his first recorded words in the story, and they are significant: "One who has waited long for you to speak."

As Lord of language, Aslan has come both to speak and to be spoken to, but what kind of words does Shasta use when he learns that the Voice in the darkness is the lion who chased him? Shasta doesn't talk at all. He "gaped with open mouth and said nothing"; then, "after one glance at the Lion's face he slipped out of the saddle and fell at its feet. He couldn't say anything but then he didn't want to say anything, and he knew he needn't say anything."

A similar silence falls on Aravis and the horses after their meeting with Aslan at the Hermit's house: "Strange to say, they felt no inclination to talk to one another about him after he had gone. They all moved slowly away to different parts of the quiet grass and there paced to and fro, each alone, thinking."

When the Mercurial Aslan gives people the gift of his word, they do not start chattering excitedly. Rather, they are moved to silence. This silence is not, however, simply an absence of words; it is an eloquent silence. This reflects the same spirit the apostle Paul writes about in the letter to the Romans: "We do not know how to pray as we ought, but the Spirit himself intercedes for us with sighs too deep for words" (Romans 8:26).

In his book on prayer, Lewis said that "prayer without words is the best," and in one of his poems, "The Apologist's Evening Prayer," he addresses God as "thou fair Silence," asking God to free him from all his excessively wordy thoughts.

This is how we should understand what happens in *The Horse and*

His Boy. Aslan, the divine Word, descends upon the children and the horses, or elevates them into his own manner of speech. The characters are thereby saved from being "dumb and witless" and are now able to communicate most truly. They speak through their behavior. Their actions speak louder than words.

Shasta says all he needs to say to Aslan when he slips out of the saddle and falls at his feet. This is a language that is lived or enacted. It is like the language Jesus spoke when he lived and died and rose again. Lewis called Christ's incarnation, crucifixion, and resurrection "a language more adequate" than any other.

After all, what are mere words if they are not filled with the Holy Spirit? Jesus taught His disciples: "In praying do not heap up empty phrases as the Gentiles do; for they think that they will be heard for their many words" (Matthew 6:7).

That Lewis never told Pauline Baynes how *The Horse and His Boy* speaks the language of Mercury should not surprise us. He was imitating something very important about God's own nature. "The Word became flesh and dwelt among us" (John 1:14). When God's Son, Jesus, was born into the world as an infant, what happened? The word *infant* literally means "speechless" (*infans* in Latin). In other words, the Word became wordless.

Lewis never *tells* us that Mercury runs throughout *The Horse and His Boy*, but the Mercurial spirit is nonetheless sounding everywhere in this brilliant story—and those who have ears to hear, let them hear!

CHAPTER NINE

APPLES ARE FROM VENUS

The Magician's Nephew

*You shall love the Lord your God with all your heart,
and with all your soul, and with all your strength,
and with all your mind.*

LUKE 10:27

IN THE BIBLE, two of the seven planets are used as symbols of Jesus Christ. We have already referred to the Sun in chapter 6. Now it is time to look at Venus, the planet of love.

Venus is especially beautiful just after dawn, and for that reason it is known as the Morning Star. It can be seen soon after sunrise gleaming like a huge diamond near the horizon.

In Revelation 22:16 Jesus says, "I am . . . the bright morning star." And earlier, in Revelation 2:28, Jesus says to the Christians in the church at Thyatira that He "will also give them the morning star" (NLT). This means He will give them Himself, the most precious gift that can be imagined.

Even earlier in the New Testament, Peter encourages the people he's writing to: "Pay close attention to what [the prophets] wrote, for their words are like a lamp shining in a dark place—until the Day dawns, and Christ the Morning Star shines in your hearts" (2 Peter 1:19, NLT).

C. S. Lewis was intrigued by these scriptural passages and refers to them in a number of places, including his great sermon "The Weight of Glory" and his novel *Perelandra*, which is set on Venus.

When writing *The Magician's Nephew*, he used Venus again, but this time secretly, turning the planet into a plot, making its symbolism a story.

To see how he did this, we need to understand the various symbolic meanings of Venus. Of the seven planets in the medieval model of the cosmos, Venus is easily the most complicated when it comes to imagery.

VENUS THE VENERABLE

To venerate something is to love it and respect it. *Venerate* is a word related to Venus because Venus was the planet especially associated with amorousness. After Aslan has sung the world of Narnia into being in *The Magician's Nephew*, his first command to the newly created animals is that they must "love."

He then shows them how they are to love, by pairing them up as male and female. Aslan walks "to and fro among the animals. And every now and then he would go up to two of them (always two at a time) and touch their noses with his. He would touch two beavers among all the beavers, two leopards among all the leopards, one stag and one deer among all the deer."

And it is not just the animals who are to love each other. The first king and queen of Narnia, Frank and Helen, are told that they will "bring up" many "children and grandchildren," that they and their "children and grandchildren shall be blessed," that they will be "father and mother of many kings."

Venus is "double-natured" (according to one of Lewis's other books), and the coupling up of these characters indicates how Aslan expects them to relate to each other. Their love is to be open, fruitful, and creative.

According to the medieval model, Venus's influence didn't just help make humanity creative and fertile: she was also creative in her own right (under God), and that is why Lewis shows Aslan creating Narnia in the way that he does in *The Magician's Nephew*:

> The Lion opened his mouth, but no sound came from it; he was breathing out, a long, warm breath; it seemed to sway all the beasts as the wind sways a line of trees. Far overhead from beyond the veil of blue sky which hid them the stars sang again; a pure, cold, difficult music. Then there came a swift flash of fire (but it burnt nobody) either from the sky or from the Lion itself, and every drop of blood tingled in the children's bodies, and the deepest, wildest voice they had ever heard was saying: "Narnia, Narnia, Narnia, awake. Love."

Have you ever wondered why "the stars sang" at the creation of Narnia? It reflects a passage from the book of Job, where God says, "Where were you when I laid the foundations of the earth. . . . when the morning stars sang together, and all the sons of God shouted for joy?" (Job 38:4, 7). Interestingly, the flash of creative fire comes "either from the sky or from the Lion." Lewis appears to be suggesting that Aslan and the singing stars of Narnia are bringing life to Narnia between them. And when the Narnian stars sing, "every drop of blood tingled in the children's bodies." Here is yet another example of Lewis making a private joke about the stars, because *tingul*, as was pointed out in an earlier chapter, is the Old English word for "star." It's a further indication that the influence of the starry heavens, and in particular the influence of Venus, the creative planet, is at work in this story.

The general theme of fruitfulness and creativity appears not only at this climactic moment when Narnia is made alive, but throughout the story—"a warm, good smell of sun-baked earth and grass and flowers," to quote some words from chapter 12 of the book.

In his poem "The Planets," Lewis wrote that Venus brings about

grass growing, and grain bursting,
Flower unfolding.

At the birth of Narnia, all these activities are mentioned, directly or indirectly.

"Grain bursting" is alluded to in the hymn the Cabby sings in the darkness, which is "all about crops being 'safely gathered in.'" The hymn is actually Henry Alford's "Come, Ye Thankful People, Come," and it contains a prayer that worshipers will be "wholesome grain and pure."

The reference to "grass growing" is more explicit than the one to grain: we are told that "the valley grew green with grass. . . . It ran up the sides of the little hills like a wave. In a few minutes it was creeping up the lower slopes of the distant mountains, making that young world every moment softer. The light wind could now be heard ruffling the grass."

And as for the "flower unfolding," we see the new grasslands "sprinkled with daisies and buttercups," while Polly notices "primroses suddenly appearing in every direction." In the newly founded Narnia, "everything is bursting with life and growth."

Venus's special relationship with creativity is suggested in the way Lewis depicts the Wood between the Worlds. Here, "you could almost feel the trees growing." It is "very much alive" and "rich and warm," "rich as plumcake," but quiet and dreamy and peaceful. It has countless pools, each giving access to a whole new creation, and this reminds us that only from such formless water "can Venus arise in her beauty," as Lewis put it in one of his academic works.

The Wood's earth is a "rich reddish brown," suggesting the presence of copper in the ground. Copper was Venus's metal. In Lewis's novel *That*

Hideous Strength, the home and garden of the hero, Ransom, are especially under the influence of Venus, and we're told in that story, quite explicitly, that "there is even copper in the soil." In *The Magician's Nephew* Lewis doesn't *explain* the Venus imagery, but he is using it nonetheless.

Venus not only produces life, she counteracts its opposite. Lewis once wrote that Venus's "union with matter—the fertility of nature—is a continual conquest of death." This brings us to the main plotline of the story: the healing of Digory's mother. Early on, Digory tells Polly that his "Mother was ill and was going to—going to—die."

Her terminal illness allows Lewis to involve Venus imagery twice. Not only can a life be saved through Venus (for, "while we ourselves can do nothing about mortality, Venus can," as Lewis wrote in another place), but the life in question is that of a mother. To Lewis, mothers signify the special combination of femininity and fertility that Venus so often symbolizes.

Mrs. Kirke's healing comes about as a result of Digory's plucking an apple from the garden in the West. And there are two key things that we should notice here. First, apples were particularly connected with Venus: they were a token of her beauty and fruitfulness. Many people think Lewis put apples into the story only because he was retelling the Genesis story of temptation. Of course, Lewis wants to make us think of the fruit of the tree of the knowledge of good and evil (Genesis 2:17), but it is also extremely important for us to know that apples are Venus's special fruit because it helps reveal the imaginative logic and atmospheric unity of *The Magician's Nephew*. (You can see a portrait of Venus with her apple on page 155.)

The other key thing about Digory's journey to find the apple is that the orchard is in the West. Why is it in the West and not the North or South or East? It's because Venus, as well as being the Morning Star, also appears in the western sky at dusk, when she is known as the Evening Star or Hesperus. *Hesperus* comes from the Greek word for "west," and in Greek mythology the Garden of the Hesperides contained a tree with apples that gave immortality.

Digory plucks the apple to protect Narnia from the evil he has brought there on the day of its birth. He does so under the watchful eye of a beautiful bird. The bird is based on a creature in a poem by John Milton (Lewis once wrote a whole book about Milton) who guards "the fair Hesperian Tree" in order "to save her blossoms, and defend her fruit / From the rash hand of bold incontinence."

After Digory has brought the apple back to Aslan and planted it, the Tree of Protection grows up in an instant. From this tree Digory is quite unexpectedly given a second apple, this one for healing his mother. After eating it, Digory's mother is able to enjoy "real, natural, gentle sleep" (or, as Jadis calls it, "sweet natural sleep"). Venus was believed to be the source of all sweetness, and it's a term Lewis frequently uses whenever he writes about her influence. For instance, in "The Planets," he mentions Venus's "breath's sweetness."

Once Digory's mother has recovered, the family piano is retuned, and the Kirke family starts playing games again. According to one of Lewis's favorite classical authors, Homer, Venus is "laughter-loving." Lewis himself once wrote that it is never wise to be "totally serious about Venus." And this helps explain why there is so much laughter throughout this story, most obviously just after the birth of Narnia, when a perky jackdaw makes "the First Joke":

> All the other animals began making various queer noises which
> are their ways of laughing and which, of course, no one has
> ever heard in our world. They tried at first to repress it, but
> Aslan said:
>
> "Laugh and fear not, creatures. Now that you are no longer
> dumb and witless, you need not always be grave. For jokes as
> well as justice come in with speech."

So they all let themselves go. And there was such merriment that the Jackdaw himself plucked up courage again and perched on the cab-horse's head, between its ears, clapping its wings, and said:

"Aslan! Aslan! Have I made the first joke? Will everybody always be told how I made the first joke?"

"No, little friend," said the Lion. "You have not *made* the first joke; you have only *been* the first joke." Then everyone laughed more than ever; but the Jackdaw didn't mind and laughed just as loud.

And laughter is found not just in Narnia. "Roars of laughter" greet Jadis when she sets herself up as an empress in London. And Jadis brings us to the other main strand of Venus imagery that we find within *The Magician's Nephew*—a much less beautiful and lovely strand.

VENUS THE VENEREAL

I pointed out that the word *venerate* (to love and respect) is related to the name *Venus*. Another related word is *venereal*. *Venereal* literally means simply "pertaining to Venus," but in modern English it is nearly always used in the term *venereal disease*. A venereal disease is usually contracted as a result of loving someone in the wrong way or at the wrong time.

For Venus, as well as symbolizing all the good, beautiful, and creative things talked about so far in this chapter, also symbolized a number of dark and joyless things. C. S. Lewis naturally knew about this shadow side to Venus, and he calls it "Venus Infernal," the hellish Venus. Interestingly, this hellish side to the Morning Star also appears in the Bible. As we have already seen, the term *Morning Star* is used several times in connection with Jesus Christ, but it is also used once in connection with evil, the exact opposite of Christ.

In the Old Testament, the prophet Isaiah speaks about the evil king of Babylon and says, "How you are fallen from heaven, O Day Star, son of Dawn!" (Isaiah 14:12). Some Bible versions translate "Day Star" as "Lucifer," which over time actually became a title for Satan.

Lewis uses the "infernal" side of the planet's imagery in the way he draws Jadis, the evil queen. Jadis speaks "the Deplorable Word" that brings death to every living thing in Charn.

Jadis's character is based on the warrior goddess Ishtar (the Babylonian Venus), who was especially worshiped by the Ninevites. This is why Jadis refers to Charn as "that great city." By having Jadis speak those words, Lewis provides an echo of Jonah's description of Nineveh as "that great city," a phrase that appears twice in the Old Testament book of Jonah (Jonah 1:2; 3:2).

Jadis is stunningly beautiful, but her beauty is hard and addictive; it makes her vain and cruel, rather than sweet and giving. When Uncle Andrew meets her, he is immediately won over by her physical attractions. He thinks "more and more of her wonderful beauty" and keeps on saying to himself, "A dem fine woman, sir, a dem fine woman. A superb creature." He imagines that "the Witch would fall in love with him," and even at the end of the book, when he is a sadder and wiser man, he is still obsessed with her and is ready to tell anyone about this "dem fine woman"—the very last words of the book.

Jadis, of course, has no time for Uncle Andrew; her selfishness is part of what makes her Venus Infernal. Also, she hates the Wood between the Worlds because it is the symbolic womb of life, and Jadis loves only death.

HEARING THE SILENT MUSIC OF VENUS

Why did Lewis build *The Magician's Nephew* out of Venus imagery? It was for two main reasons, I think.

The first is that it enabled Lewis to make Aslan sum up in his own person the venerable qualities and characteristics that appear in so much of the rest of the tale. Aslan is truly "beautiful," and Digory finds the lion's voice "beyond comparison, the most beautiful noise he had ever heard. It was so beautiful he could hardly bear it."

Aslan is also the source of sweetness. At the end of the story, Digory and Polly look up in Aslan's face and "such a sweetness and power rolled about them and over them and entered them that they felt they had never really been happy or wise or good, or even alive and awake, before." He speaks of "my sweet country of Narnia."

Aslan brings Narnia to birth like Venus, from whom "all the world derives the glorious features of beautie," "all the world by thee at first was made." (Lewis quotes these lines from the poet Spenser in one of his academic books.) "With an unspeakable thrill, [Polly] felt quite certain that all the things were coming (as she said) 'out of the Lion's head.' When you listened to his song you heard the things he was making up: when you looked round you, you saw them."

In addition to his creativity, beauty, and sweetness, Aslan orders that an apple be brought from a western garden, restores a mother's health, pairs off male and female characters, and encourages the gift of laughter. He clearly incarnates the spirit of Venus, which is everywhere in the rest of the story, just as Jesus incarnates the divine spirit that is everywhere in the real world. Lewis once wrote that God "is the reality behind . . . Venus; no woman ever conceived a child, no mare a foal, without Him."

The other main reason why Lewis structured *The Magician's Nephew* out of Venus imagery is because it enabled him to say something very important about love. Venus is "the planet of love" (as Lewis wrote in his novel *Perelandra*), and Digory must learn that his love for his mother, a love he feels to be of absolute importance, is actually only relative to his love for Aslan.

In chapter 1, we learn that Digory has been in tears because his mother is dying. She does not appear until the end of the book (chapter 15), but Digory's concern for her is repeatedly mentioned (in every chapter but 4, 5, and 8), so we don't forget that his relationship with her is the mainspring of the plot. The mixture of love and fearfulness he feels at the prospect of losing that love provides the emotional heart of this story.

This theme comes to a head when Digory is in the Western garden about to pluck the apple for Aslan. Digory has promised to fetch this apple so that a Tree of Protection can be planted that will guard Narnia from Jadis. However, Jadis tempts Digory to steal an apple and take it home to his mother so that she won't die. Digory is forced to choose between his love for Aslan and his love for his mother. He has to pluck an apple, but whom will he give it to? Aslan for the Tree of Protection or his mother for her recovery?

This is an excruciating choice, and Lewis makes clear how very painful it is: "Digory never spoke on the way back, and the others were shy of speaking to him. He was very sad and he wasn't even sure all the time that he had done the right thing; but whenever he remembered the shining tears in Aslan's eyes he became sure."

Digory keeps his promise to Aslan and brings the apple back to him. Aslan tells him that if Digory had made the wrong choice, his mother would have been healed "but not to your joy or hers. The day would have come when both you and she would have looked back and said it would have been better to die in that illness."

Digory is choked with tears as he listens, and he gives up all hope of saving his mother's life. He begins to see "that there might be things more terrible even than losing someone you love by death." In other words, he acknowledges that he could have denied his love of Aslan for the sake of clinging to his mother.

But even as he realizes how close he had come to making the wrong choice, he hears Aslan speaking again. The lion tells him to pluck a second apple, this one from the very tree he has just planted. This second apple, Aslan promises, will bring Digory's mother joy. It will not give endless life, but it will heal. "Go. Pluck her an apple from the Tree."

Lewis is illustrating the same lesson Jesus taught when He commanded His disciples to love God with all their heart and soul and mind and strength. That is the first commandment. And the second commandment is like it: "Love your neighbor as yourself" (Matthew 22:39).

When Digory allows his loves to be ordered in this way, the life, joy, and beauty of Venus become his. When Jadis steals and eats the apple, she gets her heart's desire: "She has unwearying strength and endless days like a goddess. But length of days with an evil heart is only length of misery. . . . All get what they want; they do not always like it."

If we love God the Creator above all things, we will also love His creatures, but if we love His creatures more than Him, we will find in the end that we can't love even them.

Lewis once put it very simply in a poem called "Five Sonnets," and these words, I think, provide a perfect summary of the message of *The Magician's Nephew*:

> *Ask for the Morning Star and take (thrown in)*
> *Your earthly love.*

CHAPTER TEN

SATURN'S SANDS OF TIME

The Last Battle

Time and chance happen to them all.

ECCLESIASTES 9:11

EVERYONE KNOWS THE CHARACTER of Father Time. He is an old man with a beard, carrying a scythe and an hourglass, and you can see a picture of him on page 156.

Father Time carries a scythe because he cuts people down like wheat at harvest, bringing about their deaths. And he carries an hourglass to show that our lives last only for a limited period. When the sands of time run out, our days on earth will end.

But although we all know of Father Time, hardly anybody knows that Father Time is based on the last of the seven planets. C. S. Lewis wrote in one of his academic books that Father Time "was once Saturn."

And in another place he wrote, "Our traditional picture of Father Time with the scythe is derived from earlier pictures of Saturn." Saturn was, among other things, the planet of old age, death, and disaster.

Father Time brings Narnia to an end in *The Last Battle*, helping to express the Saturnine spirit that the whole story is designed to convey.

When Jill and Eustace see this great giant, they remember having seen him asleep in the Underworld (in *The Silver Chair*) and recall "that his name was Father Time, and that he would wake on the day the world ended." If you're in any doubt that Lewis intended Father Time to represent Saturn, let me tell you what I discovered when I consulted a draft of *The Silver Chair* in Oxford University's Bodleian Library.

According to this rough draft, the Earthman in the Underworld tells Jill and Eustace when they see the figure of the sleeping giant, "That is the god Saturn, who once was a King in Over-land. . . . They say he will wake at the end of the world."

Lewis had originally planned to call Father Time *Saturn*—his intentions were going to be explicit! But when he came to publish *The Silver Chair*, he evidently changed his mind and altered *Saturn* to *Father Time* in order to keep the planetary symbolism more carefully hidden. Naturally, he kept the change of name when he wrote *The Last Battle*, the story in which Father Time finally awakes.

Lewis didn't want to make it *too* obvious that Saturn was the underlying symbol running through the final Chronicle of Narnia, but once we realize what he was up to, it is not hard to see that almost the whole tale has been structured to convey Saturn's qualities. But what are they?

Some are good; others are bad. Let's look first at the bad news.

"THE LAST PLANET, OLD AND UGLY"

According to "The Planets," Saturn is "the last planet old and ugly." Think of those three adjectives: *last, old, ugly*. They are important words in this the final Chronicle of Narnia.

Not only is the book called *The Last Battle*, but its opening sentence begins: "In the last days of Narnia . . ." The second chapter opens with the words, "About three weeks later the *last* of the Kings of Narnia . . ." Tirian is described again as "the last King" in chapters 4 and 12. In chapter 12, we hear of his "last friends" shortly after the keynote sentence of the whole story: "And then the last battle of the last King of Narnia began."

Shift the Ape is both old and ugly: "He was so old that no one could remember when he had first come to live in those parts, and he was the cleverest, ugliest, most wrinkled Ape you can imagine." Shift reappears in chapter 3, where he is described as "ten times uglier" than before. He tells the bewildered Narnians: "I'm so very old: hundreds and hundreds of years old. And it's because I'm so old that I'm so wise." Shift's great age reflects the "mountain of centuries" associated with Saturn that Lewis had written about in his novel *That Hideous Strength*: "more and still more time."

In *The Last Battle*, Father Time extinguishes the Sun by squeezing it in his hand like an orange. This reminds us of what Lewis wrote in the Saturn section of "The Planets," where he speaks of the Sun being "daunted with darkness." And it is not just the Sun that disappears in this story. All the other stars fall from the sky too. Saturn was responsible for "disastrous events," according to one of Lewis's academic books. And, as so often, Lewis chooses his words very carefully.

A disaster is, literally, a "dis-aster," a bad star. *Aster* means "star"—as in *aster*oid and *astr*onomy. Father Time brings about a "dreary and disastrous dawn" in *The Last Battle* because he is making Saturn's influence felt. Saturn was known to pre-Copernican astronomers as "The Greater Misfortune."

But we need to note that it is not just in the heavens that disaster strikes: the world of Narnia and all the characters in it have to cope with disastrous events from the very start of the story. Everyone who is alive at the beginning of this tale is dead by the end of it.

We get a hint of what's coming in chapter 1, when Shift cunningly predicts he "shall probably die" if he tries to pull out the lion skin from Caldron Pool. Puzzle retrieves it instead and is "almost tired to death" by the time he gets it out.

In chapter 2 the first actual death occurs when the dryad is cut down; then Tirian and Jewel in their anger kill two Calormenes. But to list all the deaths and references to death would be almost to retell the whole story, because the subject is everywhere.

Tirian remarks, "If we had died before today we should have been happy"; he asks, "Would it not be better to be dead than to have this horrible fear?" The Mice say, "It would have been better if we'd died before all this began." Dwarfs are taken "to die in the salt-pits of Pugrahan." One of the saddest pictures that Pauline Baynes ever drew as she illustrated the Narnia books shows Roonwit the Centaur lying dead with an arrow in his side and Cair Paravel "filled with dead Narnians."

Eventually, Tirian, Jewel, Jill, and Eustace are all forced through the Stable Door, which is "more like a mouth" than a door. And at the same time, there is a railway crash in England, causing the deaths of Peter, Edmund, Lucy, Digory, and Polly. I remember being terrified by all these events when I read them as a child. Why did Lewis include them? What is the *good* side to Saturn's influence?

HEARING THE SILENT MUSIC OF SATURN

In addition to all the terrible things that Saturn was supposed to bring about, there was one good thing. If you responded in the right way to Saturn's influence, you would gain the gift of insight. You would be able to see into the heart of things and wouldn't be deflected by superficial appearances to the contrary. In short, you would become wise.

One way in which Lewis illustrates wisdom is by showing how his good characters respond to sorrow. Sometimes they bear it without tears, and sometimes they know that crying is the right response. Jill makes sure she doesn't wet her bowstring with her tears, and Tirian doesn't show that he has given up hope even as the odds turn against him. Yet they also know when to weep freely at their losses. Lucy says that Aslan would not wish to stop them from lamenting Narnia's death. Tirian says it is no virtue to keep from mourning; not to weep would be a "discourtesy." "Blessed are those who mourn," as Jesus says in the Sermon on the Mount (Matthew 5:4).

Another way Lewis shows us wisdom is through his sketch of Narnian history in chapter 8. Jewel reminds Jill of the "hundreds and thousands of years" in Narnia's past when peaceful king followed peaceful king "till you could hardly remember their names"; he tells of Moonwood the Hare, and Swanwhite the Queen, and how King Gale obtained the Lone Islands for the Narnian kingdom:

> And as he went on, the picture of all those happy years, all the thousands of them, piled up in Jill's mind till it was rather like looking down from a high hill onto a rich, lovely plain full of woods and waters and cornfields, which spread away and away till it got thin and misty from distance.

By these means Lewis suggests not only Saturn's "mountain of centuries," but also readiness for death. The image of a rich cornfield makes us think of harvest and the approach of the natural and desirable end of life. "There is a time to be born, and a time to die," as the Old Testament book of Ecclesiastes reminds us (Ecclesiastes 3:2).

Lewis once confided to a friend that the times he most desired death were not when life was harshest: "On the contrary, it is just when there seems to be most of Heaven already here that I come nearest to longing for the *patria* [the heavenly fatherland]." Happiness on Earth "is the bright frontispiece" that encourages you to read the whole story, he said. (A frontispiece is the introductory picture at the start of a book.)

This idea of the introduction to a book appears in the final paragraph of *The Last Battle*, when we are told that the children's life in this world and all their adventures in Narnia "had only been the cover and the title page." Now "they were beginning Chapter One of the Great Story which no one on earth has read: which goes on forever: in which every chapter is better than the one before."

Lewis finishes the whole Narnia series by talking about the start of a story. It is a paradox—the opposite of what you might expect. But this paradox is just right. It expresses the good fortune that "the Greater Misfortune" brings. We all have to die. But if we are wise, we will find a new beginning even in our end.

And this is indeed what we see happen with Tirian and the other faithful Narnians. When Tirian first sees the strange, false Aslan, we are told that "horrible thoughts went through his mind." But these thoughts soon clear: Tirian "remembered the nonsense about Tash and Aslan being the same and knew that the whole thing must be a cheat."

His reaction illustrates that Saturn's influence was not evil in itself; it was evil only if you failed to make good use of it. As his kingdom is brought to its appointed end, Tirian makes good use of Saturnine influence by looking beyond surface realities with a wise spiritual insight.

The biblical passage that appears most frequently in Lewis's writings is Jesus Christ's cry from the cross: "My God, my God, why hast thou forsaken me?" (Matthew 27:46 and Mark 15:34, quoting Psalm 22:1). In fact, Lewis refers to this Scripture more often than any other passage by a large margin.

The cry from the cross is echoed in *The Last Battle* when Tirian cries out from the tree, where he stands bound and bleeding:

And he called out, "Aslan! Aslan! Aslan! Come and help us now."

But the darkness and the cold and the quietness went on just the same.

Though he receives no reply, Tirian continues with his prayer:

"Let *me* be killed," cried the King. "I ask nothing for myself. But come and save all Narnia."

And still there was no change in the night or the wood, but there began to be a kind of change inside Tirian. Without knowing why, he began to feel a faint hope. And he felt somehow stronger.

Tirian's circumstances don't change, but his attitude does. Aslan does not "come and help" in the way Tirian wants, but the king is stronger for calling on him.

Jewel the Unicorn also remains faithful. He trusts that the stable "may be for us the door to Aslan's country and we shall sup at his table tonight."

Lewis is trying to teach us about true faith—"the conviction of things not seen" (Hebrews 11:1). Tirian sees Aslan with the eyes of his heart, even though Aslan does not appear in the story in person until after Tirian's life in Narnia has come to its end.

Tirian says, "In the name of Aslan let us go forward"; "I serve the real Aslan." He resolves to take "the adventure that Aslan would send," for "we are all between the paws of the true Aslan"; "Aslan to our aid!" As a result, after death, Tirian finally gets to see Aslan and hear him say: "Well done, last of the Kings of Narnia who stood firm at the darkest hour."

Emeth, the Calormene soldier, is another example of someone with wise faith. *Emeth* is a Hebrew word meaning "fidelity, truth, permanence," so the soldier's very name suggests he is a true child of Saturn.

We are also told that Emeth is a "seventh son." (Tirian, too, is said to be "seventh in descent" from King Rilian.) As Saturn, the seventh planet, exerts his influence, Emeth is welcomed into the heavenly Narnia. Aslan tells Emeth that he has been worshiping him all his life, even though he never realized it. Emeth's heart has been with Aslan, despite all appearances to the contrary.

And what happens with Tirian and Emeth is also meant to happen to us as we read the story. We are expected to keep trusting in Aslan, even though he does not appear. And if we have eyes to see him, we can find Aslan in the story despite his absence.

The water from the white rock that refreshes everyone during the battle is a hint that Aslan is still in control. (It reminds us of the Christlike rock in the desert referred to in 1 Corinthians 10:4). The sweet and piercing innocence of the Lamb in chapter 3 reminds us that Christ Himself is "the Lamb of God" (John 1:29).

Perhaps most importantly of all, Roonwit the Centaur says near the start of the story that he has seen "disastrous conjunctions of the planets." This is terrible news for Narnia, because it foretells the end of the world, but it is also reassuring news because "the stars never lie."

Aslan, as Jewel points out, "is not the slave of the stars but their Maker." Aslan has made the stars, and the stars tell the truth. Even though the truth they tell is a hard and painful one, Aslan is still their Maker. He is working his purposes out.

TINGLING ALL OVER

And what is Aslan's final purpose? It is to bring the children to himself. The pain and the suffering of the story are not where the story ends. Saturn's influence is not final. In Lewis's poem "The Planets," Saturn is not the stopping point. The poem goes beyond the sphere of Saturn and looks past the edge of the sky into "Heaven's hermitage."

"Heaven's hermitage"—the Heaven where Aslan lives—is the goal of the whole story. And once the children break through into this heavenly Narnia, we can see that Saturn's influence has begun to fade. Jupiter, the joyful king, is taking over again.

The spirit of the sixth sphere, Jupiter, is also the spirit that governs the universe *beyond* the seventh in the resurrection home of Aslan. In Lewis's works, Saturn always gives way to Jupiter, whose qualities Lewis thought better represented the heart of spiritual reality. In *That Hideous Strength* Saturn is "overmatched" by Jupiter. In Lewis's poem "The Turn of the Tide," wintry Saturn is defrosted by the Jovial birth of Christ at Bethlehem.

In the last quarter of *The Last Battle*, Lewis symbolizes the same thing. While the first two-thirds take us to Tirian's death, in the closing section, Saturn withdraws (so to speak) and Jupiter comes to the fore.

Digory and Polly become "unstiffened" and no longer feel old. Edmund's sore knee is healed. Erlian's grey-haired head regains its youthful color. Caldron Pool, once "bitingly cold," now turns to a "delicious foamy coolness." We hear a mention of "the summer sea"; the air gently blowing on the heroes' faces "was that of a day in early summer."

And there are certain, even more obvious indications that Saturn is no longer at the center of the stage. One of these occurs when Jove is mentioned directly:

> "Isn't it wonderful?" said Lucy. "Have you noticed one can't feel afraid, even if one wants to? Try it."
>
> "By Jove, neither one can," said Eustace after he had tried.

And so we see that Saturn has brought about the very best thing, the return to the Jovial spirit of *The Lion, the Witch and the Wardrobe*. Saturn enables the children to see beyond sorrow. Saturn, like Luna, Mercury, Venus, Sol, and Mars, is a servant of Jupiter.

Jovial happiness is at the heart of the Narnian universe, and in the end, the characters who appear in *The Last Battle* have to decide which they prefer: Jovial happiness or Saturnine sorrow. (Susan doesn't appear in the story, so we aren't told what happens to her; however, in a letter to a reader, Lewis writes that perhaps Susan will get to Narnia in the end.)

The Dwarfs choose sorrow. They are what Lewis elsewhere calls "Saturnocentric," their minds fixed on Saturn, unable to get beyond the grimness and darkness he represents. But the children and the others who keep the faith are overwhelmed with joy: for them, everything sad becomes untrue.

> "Further in and higher up!" cried Roonwit. . . . And though
> they did not understand him, the words somehow set them
> tingling all over.

The effect of the centaur's cry indicates that the end of their adventures has at last been reached. "Tingling," as has been pointed out several times in this book, is Lewis's private way of referring to the influence of the stars. The "tingling" is now complete, and it is time for every friend of Narnia to enter into joy.

Lewis said that, for Dante, "the gathering of the Church Triumphant in Heaven" was "the fruit of Time, or of the Spheres." In *The Divine Comedy*, the hero of the story stands on the brink of Paradise and looks back across all the seven heavens that he has traveled through during his journey to God's home. In *The Last Battle*, Lewis does something similar.

He looks back across all the stories and summons onto the page characters from all seven of the planetary realms: Tumnus from his Jupiter story, Reepicheep from his Mars world, the hopping Monopods from Sol, Puddleglum from the Moon, Cor and Corin from Mercury, Frank and Helen from Venus, Tirian and Jewel from Saturn. This is the Narnian equivalent of "the fruit of Time or of the Spheres." All the friends of Narnia gather in Aslan's country to begin the story in which every chapter is better than the one before.

But why does it matter that Lewis used the symbolism of the planetary spheres for his Narnia Chronicles? What does it add to our appreciation of these books to know that he wrote them this way? These are the questions we will try to answer in the next chapter.

CHAPTER ELEVEN

THE CANDLESTICK

*I saw a gold menorah with seven branches,
and in the center, the Son of Man.*

REVELATION 1:12-13

LEWIS SAID THAT THE Chronicles of Narnia are "about Christ." What I have tried to show in the last ten chapters is *how* they are about Christ.

When Lewis used the word *Christ*, he didn't just mean Jesus of Nazareth, the historical figure who lived in Palestine two thousand years ago. He also meant the Son of God, God the Son, through whom all things were made and in whom all things hold together.

Lewis took the seven heavens that he so loved and used them as symbols of Christ. And because the seven planets symbolize Christ, they also symbolize everything He made. They have to, because there is a connection between Christ and creation. As Lewis said, "[Christ] is the all-pervasive principle of concretion or cohesion whereby the universe holds together."

So when we read *The Lion, the Witch and the Wardrobe*, we shouldn't *just* think, *Aslan is like Christ because he dies for Edmund* and leave it at that. Of course, it is true and very important that Aslan is like Christ because he dies for Edmund. But there is so much more going on. The books are much *more* Christian than we've realized!

Imagine you're C. S. Lewis. You want to have a Christ figure in your story. You want to show Christ dying for His people. You want to show the people becoming obedient to Christ. You want to show that the whole world is Christ's. How do you do this?

Lewis did it by means of Jupiter imagery because Jupiter's imagery was extensive enough to let him do all these things at once. Aslan is the royal King of the Wood. Aslan's blood shed for Edmund is like the Great Red Spot "bleeding" on kingly Jupiter. Narnia is freed from the Witch's winter and becomes able to celebrate the "jollification" of Christmas once again. The children are all crowned as kings or queens at the end of the adventure. And so on and so forth.

The Jovial imagery runs under and through all these aspects of the story, shaping them and binding them together. There is a spirit linking all these different things just as in the real world the Spirit of Christ is to be seen both in the Creator and in His creation.

It was a very skillful and subtle thing that Lewis did. And I think it helps explain why the Narnia Chronicles have become so popular. Although it wasn't clear before now *how* he made the stories hold together, I think we have sensed that they *do* hold together. We have felt it in our bones. We have thought, *There's more going on here than meets the eye.*

Let's quickly review how Lewis uses the seven heavens, those "spiritual symbols" of "permanent value," as he called them.

- In *The Lion, the Witch and the Wardrobe*, the children become kings and queens under the royal crown of Jupiter.
- In *Prince Caspian*, they become knights and forest folk under the wooden shield of Mars.
- In *The Voyage of the "Dawn Treader,"* they drink light and slay dragons under the Sun's golden embrace.
- In *The Silver Chair*, they avoid lunacy and reflect truth beneath the mirroring Moon.
- In *The Horse and His Boy*, they learn true speech under the living and active word of Mercury.
- In *The Magician's Nephew*, they witness creation, laugh, and learn to love the Morning Star.
- And in *The Last Battle*, under Saturn's awful and awe-full influence, they learn the final lesson: "Blessed are those who die in the Lord" (Revelation 14:13, NLT).

The children and we, the readers, "look along" these influences. We "enjoy" the heavenly atmosphere in each book—breathing it, smelling it, tasting it, allowing it to fill and inform our whole imaginative experience.

And we do so seven times over.

When I think about the seven Chronicles and how Lewis uses each planet to say something about Christ, I'm reminded of the verse, "I saw a gold menorah with seven branches, and in the center, the Son of Man" (Revelation 1:12-13, THE MESSAGE).

The Son of Man, Christ, is the focal point of this seven-branched candlestick. He is at the heart of all illumination, just as Aslan is "at the back of all the stories," according to Shasta in *The Horse and His Boy*.

But why have seven stories rather than just one? Why would Lewis want to repeat himself?

THE NARNIA CODE

SEVEN STARS FOR SEVEN STORIES

When he began writing *The Lion, the Witch and the Wardrobe*, Lewis didn't know there was going to be more than one book. He wanted to write a Jupiter-themed story, I believe, because Jupiter was his favorite planet, the one he jokingly said he himself had been born under, and the one he thought the people needed to know about more than any other. "Of Saturn we know more than enough," he said, "but who does not need to be reminded of Jove?"

Having written his Jove story, Lewis then started work on his Venus tale (*The Magician's Nephew*), but he couldn't find the right shape for that story, so he set it aside for a while.

In the meantime, he wrote *Prince Caspian* and *The Voyage of the "Dawn Treader,"* and it was around then that he decided he would do all seven. He had actually finished four of the books before he published the first. *The Lion, the Witch and the Wardrobe* was published in 1950, and the other six followed, one each year, until 1956.

He told one of his former students that he had had "an idea" that he wanted to try out, and now, having "tried it out to the full" after seven books, it was time to stop.

In the course of writing the series, Lewis was able to present Christ in seven different ways. Aslan is King, Commander, Light, Mirror, Word, Life, and Mystery. Lewis thought it was important to speak about Christ in many different ways because no one way, on its own, was enough. Why are there four Gospels in the Bible? Each one gives a particular perspective on Jesus' life and ministry. The same is true of the seven heavens. Each planet provides its own unique way of representing the spiritual life.

Lewis once said that an image of Christ is only "a model or symbol, certain to fail us in the long run and, even while we use it, requiring correction from other models." These symbols will fail us in the long run because they are only *symbols*; they are not the thing itself. Only

Christ Himself never fails. We have to think about Christ using ideas and images, but if we put our trust in these symbols, rather than in the One they symbolize, we will be making a big mistake.

"You shall not make for yourself a graven image." So says the second of the Ten Commandments. A graven image needn't just mean a literal idol made out of wood or stone. It might also mean a mental idol, an image in the mind. We can make our own thoughts into idols and worship our ideas of God as if *they* were God. But, as Lewis once said, "My idea of God is not a divine idea."

By using more than one image for God, we remind ourselves that any image we use is only temporary; it must be corrected and relieved by other images. These images serve our minds; they do not save our souls. A fork is not food.

CONSIDER THE HEAVENS

And what is true of our thinking about God is also true of our thinking about the universe. Our models of the cosmos are also temporary. They come and they go.

Until the time of Copernicus, people believed that the Earth was static and central. Following Copernicus, we believe that the sun is the center and the Earth moves round it.

And since the Copernican Revolution, there have been other great changes in the ways we think about the universe. Our map of the cosmos has been altered significantly by the discoveries and theories of Sir Isaac Newton and Albert Einstein, to mention just two of the greatest physicists.

In due course, other great astronomers and physicists will come along with new ideas, causing us to rethink our understanding of the universe and our place in it. For that reason, it makes sense to hold our understanding lightly. We shouldn't cling too tightly to any one model or image. And neither should we throw away any image too emphatically.

This is the point that Lewis was trying to make in *The Discarded Image*. He was saying, "Don't completely forget the pre-Copernican cosmos! Don't discard it too hastily!" The pre-Copernican model is outdated in many ways, but not in every way. It won't enable you to fly to the moon, but it will help you think about the moon in rich and meaningful ways.

We don't just want to know how far away the moon is and what it's made of and how much it weighs. We also want to find the *spiritual* significance of the moon. The pre-Copernican way of thinking about the planets kept in mind their spiritual purpose and qualities. That old way of thinking may not have always come up with the right answers, but it was asking very good questions. Lewis wonders whether the questions of modern science are the best or only sorts of questions to be asked. In *The Discarded Image*, he says this:

> I hope no one will think that I am recommending a return to
> the Medieval Model. I am only suggesting considerations that
> may induce us to regard all Models in the right way, respecting
> each and idolising none.

And as so often, Lewis is making a quiet joke here. The joke is to be found in his use of the word *considerations*. *Consider* comes from two Latin words—*con*, meaning "with," and *sidus*, meaning "star." To consider something means not just to think about it but to think about it "with the stars." It was originally a term used in astrology. But how many people are even aware of the origin and meaning of the word? We have forgotten that old way of thinking.

We are, in fact, poorer than our ancestors in this respect because we no longer understand so many of the terms we use—not only *consider*, but also *tingle* and *commerce* and *influenza* and *venerable* and *lunatic* and *disaster*. We have forgotten why March is called March!

If we don't understand where we have come from, we won't really understand where we are or where we're going. It's vital to keep alive a knowledge of old ways of thinking in order to keep fully alive our *present* way of thinking.

And it's not just in *The Discarded Image* that Lewis uses the word *consider* with an awareness of its old meaning. In *That Hideous Strength*, Mercury descends to Earth and inspires people to make puns and play with words: "paradoxes, fancies, anecdotes, theories laughingly advanced yet (on consideration) well worth taking seriously." The appearance of the word *consideration* in this passage is itself a pun!

And Lewis uses it again in *The Lion, the Witch and the Wardrobe*. Peter and Susan are worried that Lucy might be going crazy. She has claimed that there is a magic world behind the wardrobe, but they can't find it when they go looking. So Peter and Susan take their concerns to the professor. He asks them how they know that Lucy's story isn't true and Susan replies, "But Edmund said they had only been pretending."

"That is a point," the professor says, "which certainly deserves consideration; very careful consideration."

If we understand Lewis's love of words and his love of the planets, we will see that the professor means more by this than at first appears. Peter and Susan must give "careful consideration" to what Edmund says. Edmund has been to the magic world but pretends he hasn't. When Peter and Susan fully *consider* the situation—when they think and act "with the stars" and, in particular, when they act in a Jovial way—they will discover the truth.

"O-o-oh!" said Susan suddenly. And everyone asked her what was the matter.

"I'm sitting against a tree," said Susan, "and look! It's getting light—over there."

"By Jove, you're right," said Peter, "and look there—and there. It's trees all round. And this wet stuff is snow. Why, I do believe we've got into Lucy's wood after all."

"By Jove," says Peter, not realizing the full significance of what he has just said! But it is by Jove (that is, by God symbolized as Jove) that he can see the truth of the world beyond the wardrobe.

To think "with the stars" means to think spiritually, to remember that the material world is more than just matter. Modern science is brilliant at answering questions that begin with "what" or "where" or "how." *What* are the stars made of? *Where* are they located? *How* do they move? But there are other questions that are worth asking too. Questions that begin with "why" and "who" and "whom." *Why* have the stars been made? *Who* made them? *Whom* were they made for?

Modern science tends to think only in terms of matter and mechanism and measurements. But pre-Copernican science tended to think also in terms of purposes and points and persons. Lewis thought it was a mistake to allow the two sets of questions to get split apart from each other. To be fully human we need to ask and try to answer both sets of questions, not just one set.

Here it's worth repeating the brief conversation between Eustace and Ramandu in *The Voyage of the "Dawn Treader"*:

"In our world," said Eustace, "a star is a huge ball of flaming gas."

"Even in your world, my son, that is not what a star is but only what it is made of."

When we fully consider what a star is, we will see that it is more than just its material parts—if we have eyes to see. A star is a messenger of divine creativity—if we have ears to hear.

But how can we see something invisible? How can we hear the silent music of the spheres? That leads us to the subject of our final chapter.

CHAPTER TWELVE

THE TELESCOPE

For now we see through a glass, darkly;
but then face to face.

I CORINTHIANS 13:12

C. S. Lewis had a telescope on the balcony of his bedroom and liked visiting the local observatory in Oxford where he lived. He often pointed out unusual conjunctions of the planets to his friends or wrote letters to people mentioning what he had recently been observing in the sky.

For instance, he once wrote to his godson, Laurence Harwood (the godson to whom he sent coded messages), and asked him, "Do you ever notice Venus these mornings at about quarter past seven? She has been terrifically bright lately, almost better than Jupiter."

But it is one thing to observe the planets; it is another thing to see them as divine messengers—to hear them "telling the glory of God" (Psalm 19:1).

How can we see them in that way or hear their silent music?

Here is where we come back to the discovery of Neptune by the astronomer John Couch Adams. (His middle name is pronounced "Cooch," by the way.) He was sitting in his Cambridge observatory one day, thinking. And what he was thinking about was the planet Uranus. He was wondering why Uranus orbited the Sun the way it did. The orbit wasn't quite as he would have expected. There was a kink in it.

Adams realized that there must be another planet *beyond* Uranus, exerting a gravitational pull on it and pulling it slightly out of a smooth orbit around the Sun. And the amazing thing is that Adams correctly worked out not only the existence of Neptune but also its position before he ever saw it!

Neptune floats in the sky about two and a half billion miles above the Earth. And yet John Couch Adams knew it was there even without observing it. How did he know this? By correctly using reason, logic, and mathematics.

Lewis thought that this was an astounding achievement and wrote about it in his book *Miracles*. He saw it as evidence that the universe is filled with the spirit of reason. Our minds, working properly, can plug into this spirit of reason and work out all sorts of mysteries, even in the remotest corners of the universe.

But imagine if you'd been sitting in the observatory *next* to John Couch Adams while he had been thinking those great thoughts. You would have looked at him and seen just an ordinary man with an ordinary-sized head. Yet inside that head the gigantic planet of Neptune, billions of miles away, was making itself known.

If a brain scanner had existed back then, it could have recorded certain electrical impulses as Adams's brain worked away. But from the inside, from Adams's point of view, the electrical impulses would not have been electrical impulses; they would have been ideas flooded with meaning, with mighty wonders of the night sky.

Which viewpoint is more valuable? The outside one, which sees little movements of grey matter, or the inside one, which perceives a whole new heavenly body? Lewis would have said that Adams's viewpoint was more valuable. Adams was inside the experience, looking along the beam of reason. And what Adams achieved by standing within the light of reason is a good picture of what a Christian does when he or she stands within the light of faith.

Once your mind is plugged into the Holy Spirit of God, you can begin to see that the heavens declare His glory. And how can you get plugged into God's Spirit? In order to know God, what do you have to do?

Adams plugged himself into the spirit of reason by working hard, thinking clearly, and reading widely. He made himself into a good astronomer. To know God, must we also do the right things and live cleanly and be good people? Yes and no.

On the one hand, no. Lewis puts it like this:

> When you come to knowing God, the initiative lies on His side. If He does not show Himself, nothing you can do will enable you to find Him. And, in fact, He shows much more of Himself to some people than to others—not because He has favourites, but because it is impossible for Him to show Himself to a man whose whole mind and character are in the wrong condition. Just as sunlight, though it has no favourites, cannot be reflected in a dusty mirror as clearly as in a clean one.

Nothing we can do will enable us to find God if God doesn't want us to find Him. Caspian in *The Voyage of the "Dawn Treader"* has to realize that he can't get to Aslan's country unless and until Aslan chooses to call him there. To put this in theological language, we would say that it is only by God's grace that we can be saved—only because God freely draws us to Himself through the sacrificial death of Christ are we able to come to Him. He calls us because He loves us, not because we merit the call.

But on the other hand, yes, we do need to work hard and try to be good and true and beautiful people. Why? Because God wants us to be people like that: the more we are like that, the more we will be able to respond to His love. Aslan *was* calling Caspian, but *via* his life in Narnia. Aslan wanted Caspian to live his life in Narnia in a way that would prepare him for Aslan's country later. Caspian's whole life—his well-lived life—was the route he had to travel in order to arrive in Aslan's country at the end of *The Silver Chair*.

In other words, Aslan wanted Caspian to be perfect—to clean the dust off his mirror, to remove the smudges from his telescope—not because these things would earn Caspian the right to enter Aslan's country, but because they were part of what Caspian, as someone destined for Aslan's country, would naturally want and need to do.

Lewis puts it like this:

> While in other sciences the instruments you use are things external to yourself (things like microscopes and telescopes), the instrument through which you see God is your whole self. And if a man's self is not kept clean and bright, his glimpse of God will be blurred—like the Moon seen through a dirty telescope.

The only problem is this: we can't keep ourselves clean and bright! We keep getting our telescopes dirty. That's why we need other people to help us—other Christians who will guide us and encourage us and rebuke us. We need to pray together and read the Bible together and eat the Lord's Supper together.

Lewis writes:

The one really adequate instrument for learning about
God is the whole Christian community, waiting for Him
together. Christian brotherhood is, so to speak, the technical
equipment for this science—the laboratory outfit. That is
why all these people who turn up every few years with some
patent simplified religion of their own as a substitute for the
Christian tradition are really wasting time. Like a man who has
no instrument but an old pair of field glasses setting out to put
all the real astronomers right. He may be a clever chap—he
may be cleverer than some of the real astronomers, but he is
not giving himself a chance. And two years later everyone has
forgotten all about him, but the real science is still going on.

It is humiliating to realize that we need other people; we would like
to be self-sufficient. It is humiliating to realize that we can't find God
unless God wants to be found; we would prefer it if He would be at our
beck and call. But these humiliations are necessary if we are to make
any progress at all.

THE NARNIA CODE

Let me finish this book by telling you a little bit more about how I discovered the Narnia code. It is worth recounting because it illustrates our
need for other people and our need for an act of revelation in the life of
faith. I have already told you of the eureka moment when I was reading
"The Planets" in bed, but now I need to tell you what happened earlier
that week and earlier that day.

Earlier that week, a friend of mine, Christopher Holmwood, gave
me the soundtrack to the Royal Shakespeare Company's production of
The Lion, the Witch and the Wardrobe. I listened to it several times in

just a few days, and although I didn't like every track, I thought some numbers interpreted parts of the story extremely well. In any event, the recording caused me to immerse myself in Lewis's story *as told through music*. If you like, I was beginning to listen to its heart, to tune into its spirit. I was hearing Lewis's story, but hearing it without words.

A few days later I had a meeting in Cambridge with the Right Reverend Simon Barrington-Ward, the former Bishop of Coventry. Bishop Simon knew Lewis well in the 1950s. Long before he became a bishop, he worked as chaplain of Magdalene College, Cambridge, during the time when Lewis was there as professor of medieval and Renaissance literature. The two men used to go walking together and spoke with one another at quite a close, personal level despite the difference in their ages.

After Lewis resigned his position because of ill health, he wrote to the master of Magdalene College, jokingly saying that he would haunt the college buildings and grounds, but only because he loved the place so much. And he made a particular reference to his young friend, the college chaplain, saying, "If in some twilit hour anyone sees a bald and bulky spectre in the Combination Room or the garden, don't get Simon to exorcise it, for it is a harmless wraith and means nothing but good."

In my meeting with Bishop Simon on this occasion, I asked him to help me understand what Lewis meant by "wordless prayer," a subject Lewis talks about quite a bit in his book on prayer, *Letters to Malcolm*. I wasn't sure what wordless prayer was, and I couldn't understand why Lewis, who was so gifted with words, would want (or need) to pray without them.

In order to help me understand this point, Bishop Simon opened up a book called *The Monk of Mount Athos* and read aloud a passage describing a meeting between two monks, an old monk and a young monk.

The old monk was wise and eloquent, full of his own intelligence. But he suddenly found that he had nothing to say when the younger monk, in all simplicity, asked him, "How do the perfect speak?" The older monk realized he didn't know the first thing about perfect speech. But his inability to speak allowed him to hear, and into his humbled silence the young monk planted the message that "The perfect never say anything of themselves. . . . They only say what the Spirit suffers them to say."

The point that the younger monk was making was basically the same point Paul makes in his letter to the Romans where he explains how the Holy Spirit "intercedes for us with sighs too deep for words" (Romans 8:26). When the Holy Spirit truly breathes through human prayers, words aren't always needed.

As Simon read this passage aloud, it made an extraordinarily deep impact on me. There was a momentous charge in the words, and the atmosphere in the room suddenly became intense and rich.

After this most unusual experience, I returned to my theological college, Ridley Hall, in a kind of daze. I did not know exactly what had happened to me, but I felt certain it was somehow tremendously important.

Before going to sleep that night, I lay in bed reading Lewis's chapter on "The Heavens" in *The Discarded Image*. The thought occurred to me that it would be useful to compare Lewis's academic understanding of the heavens with his poetic treatment of the same thing.

That was when I pulled out my copy of his collected poems and began reading "The Planets." The phrase "winter passed / And guilt forgiven" sprang from the page, demanding my attention. I had come across the passing of winter and the forgiving of guilt elsewhere in Lewis's writings: those things formed the centerpiece of his first Narnia tale. Could there be a link somehow between the poem and Chronicle? That thought was the stray spark connecting Jupiter to *The Lion, the Witch and the Wardrobe* in my mind, and one by one the other planet-to-book relationships began to follow.

As the whole pattern began to come clear and make sense, I remembered my conversation with Simon Barrington-Ward. The young monk had talked about the Holy Spirit speaking through human prayers. Here in Lewis's fiction was an imaginative version of a similar sort of thing: spiritual symbols speaking through stories.

I immediately knew, though it took much longer to understand fully and reliably, that Lewis had cryptically designed the Chronicles so that the seven heavens spoke through them like a kind of language or song. He had translated the planets into plots, and the music of the spheres could be heard silently sounding (or tingling, as he would have said) in each tale.

The Narnia series, I now started to see, was a literary equivalent of Holst's *Planets Suite*; each one of the seven heavens gave the key to a different Chronicle.

When as a child I made my silhouette pictures of a lion, a witch, and a wardrobe, I had typed "cslewiscslewiscslewis" back and forth across each image. What I really should have typed was "jupiterjupiterjupiter." That was the signature tune sounding throughout the whole work. I had never literally heard it, and yet I *had* heard it every time I read the book.

THE END

The Narnia code, as I've called it, was a brilliant idea of Lewis's, and discovering it helps explain all sorts of fascinating and beautiful things about the seven stories. But I think Lewis would want us to concentrate not on him and his Chronicles, but on God and His creation.

Lewis described Psalm 19 as the greatest poem in the book of Psalms and one of the greatest lyrics in the entire world. The apostle Paul quotes Psalm 19 and says that what the heavens speak is "the word of Christ" (Romans 10:17-18, NIV). So let us finish with the opening verses of that psalm:

The heavens are telling the glory of God;
    and the firmament proclaims his handiwork.
Day to day pours forth speech,
    and night to night declares knowledge.
There is no speech, nor are there words;
    their voice is not heard;
yet their voice goes out through all the earth,
    and their words to the end of the world.   PSALM 19:1-4

In his book *Cosmographia*, published in 1585, astronomer Peter Apian included this diagram illustrating the pre-Copernican universe. The seven planets are shown orbiting the Earth in the following order: Luna (Moon), Mercury, Venus, Sol (Sun), Mars, Jupiter (sometimes called Jove), Saturn. It is these seven planets that give us the names of the days of the week.

This woodcut by Hans Sebald Beham (1500–1550) portrays Jupiter enthroned in the heavens and some of his influences on earth. Jupiter inspires coronation (foreground), judgment (middle left), and hunting (background). (Photo: Warburg Institute.) *The Lion, the Witch and the Wardrobe* is a Jovial story full of kings and queens, forgiveness, the passing of winter, and the hunting of white stags.

This fresco, located in the Casa di Venere in Pompeii, shows Mars in his capacities as god of war (Mars Gradivus) and god of woods (Mars Silvanus). *Prince Caspian* is a Martial story, full of trees and forests, battles and knights, including that most knightly figure, Reepicheep, the "martial mouse."

Apollo, the god of light or the sun, was sometimes known as Sauroctonus, the slayer of lizards or dragons. This is a copy of a bronze statue from the fourth century BC by Praxiteles, in the Vatican Museum in Rome. (Photo: Warburg Institute.) *The Voyage of the "Dawn Treader"* is a Solar story, full of sunlight, gold, and adventures with dragons.

Luna, the moon goddess, in her chariot that she drives across the heavens, marking the boundary between the constancy above and the confusion below. Bas relief in the Malatestian Temple, Rimini, Italy, created about 1470. (Photo: Warburg Institute.) *The Silver Chair* is a Lunar story, full of wanderings, wetness, silver, lunacy, and the horses Coalback and Snowflake.

Mercury, the winged messenger, is the subject of this copy of a statue by Giovanni da Bologna (c. 1524–1608), which was erected in Tom Quad, Christ Church, Oxford, in 1928. (Photo: Michael Ward; used by permission of Christ Church.) *The Horse and His Boy* is a Mercurial story, full of running heralds, wordy characters, winged caps, and comings and goings.

Venus, source of sweetness, creativity, and laughter, holds an apple in this oil painting by Bartholomeus van der Helst (1613–1670), located in the Musée des Beaux-Arts near Lille, France. *The Magician's Nephew* is a Venereal story in which Narnia is created, the first joke is told, and a magic apple brings life and health.

This sculpture was created by John Flanagan (1865–1952) and stands in the Library of Congress in Washington, D.C. (Photo: Carol Highsmith.) "Our traditional picture of Father Time with his scythe is derived from earlier pictures of Saturn," Lewis writes in *The Discarded Image*. *The Last Battle* is a Saturnine story in which Father Time brings Narnia to an end.

"We have seen his star in the East, and have come to worship him" (Matthew 2:2). The story of the Wise Men's visit to the baby Jesus is just one of many biblical examples of the way "the heavens are telling the glory of God" (Psalm 19:1). (Illustration: Gustave Dore, The Dore Bible Illustrations.)

ACKNOWLEDGMENTS

I GRATEFULLY ACKNOWLEDGE the help and kindness of the following people:

The many readers of *Planet Narnia* and viewers of *The Narnia Code* documentary who suggested a book of this sort; in particular, Robin Parry of Paternoster Press, who e-mailed me out of the blue with an unsolicited commission—an author's dream.

Kim Miller, Sarah Atkinson, and Jonathan Schindler at Tyndale for their excellent editorial work.

Cynthia Read of Oxford University Press for permission to abridge and refashion *Planet Narnia* as *The Narnia Code*.

Walter Hooper for his endless encouragements and especially for pointing out the Saturn reference in the one surviving Narnia typescript.

Bernard O'Donoghue of Wadham College, Oxford, for showing me Lewis's astrological marginalia in his complete edition of Chaucer.

The late Pauline Baynes for responding to my inquiries about her Narnia illustrations.

The staff of the Bodleian Library, Oxford, and the Wade Center, Wheaton College, Illinois, for their superb archival assistance.

Christopher Holmwood and Bishop Simon Barrington-Ward for their parts in the discovery that led to this book.

Members of the Oxford Lewis Society, especially the president, David Baird, for spurring this project toward fruition.

Fr. Andrew Cuneo, the first person to gain an Oxford doctorate on Lewis, for his scholarly advice and personal support.

Davey Talbot of Davey's Daily Poetry for illuminating Lewis's Mercurial wordplay.

Norman Stone of 1A Productions for directing *The Narnia Code* documentary.

The C. S. Lewis Foundation, owners of The Kilns, for their continual hospitality.

William Clayton of williamclayton.com for the author photo.

Mark Dodwell of mkdynamic for designing www.narniacode.com.

Greg Anderson, Sarah Arthur, Anne Atkins, David Beckmann, Steve Beebe, Paul Bootes, Justin Brierley, David Brooks, Keith Carlson, David Crouse, Salim Firth, Mike Gilbart-Smith, Malcolm Guite, Charles Hart, Louis Hemmings, Alan Jacobs, Karl Johnson, Paul Kerry, Kalman Kingsley, Roger Laing, Chip Lind, Theodore Roosevelt Malloch, Doug Mantha, Wayne Martindale, Eric Metaxas, Kenneth Myers, Alan Noake, Jamie Parker, James Patrick, Elizabeth Peters, J. A. C. Redford, Mike Reeves, Mark Rigg, Doug Robinson, Jerry Root, Phil Ryken, John Seel, Mark Sommer, Charlie Starr, Dick Staub, William Tate, David Theroux, Tom Wright, John Yates III—all of whom, in various memorable ways, smoothed the path from *Planet Narnia* to *The Narnia Code*.

And finally, Chris Cuneo, who set up a telescope in the backyard of his house in Jupiter, Florida, and said, "You've never looked through a 'scope? Look through that!" I did so and saw Jupiter, 365 million miles away.

Michael Ward
St. Peter's College, Oxford
Feast of St. Peter, 2010

NOTES

CHAPTER 1: THE MYSTERY

2 *strikes the wrong note:* Donald E. Glover, *C. S. Lewis: The Art of Enchantment* (Athens, OH: Ohio University Press, 1981), 141.

2 *incongruous:* Clyde S. Kilby, *The Christian World of C. S. Lewis* (Abingdon: Marcham Manor Press, 1965), 145.

2 *to be true . . . taking it into Narnia:* Peter J. Schakel, *Reading with the Heart: The Way into Narnia,* 140.

4 *about Christ:* C. S. Lewis, Letter to Anne Jenkins, March 5, 1961, in *Collected Letters,* Vol. 3, 1244.

4 *In* The Silver Chair . . . *"God with us":* Although Aslan appears alongside Jill and Eustace at the end of the story, it is actually their location that has changed, not his. See my *Planet Narnia,* 132–133.

4 *swift of foot:* C. S. Lewis, *The Horse and His Boy,* 164.

5 *which goes on forever . . . better than the one before:* C. S. Lewis, *The Last Battle,* 211.

6 *jumble . . . full of inconsistencies:* A. N. Wilson, *C. S. Lewis: A Biography* (New York: W. W. Norton & Co., 1990), 225.

6 *uneven . . . hastily written:* Humphrey Carpenter, *The Inklings,* 224–227.

6 *glibly . . . whizz-bang, easy-come-easy-go, slap-it-down kind of way:* Brian Sibley, *Cover Stories,* BBC Radio 4 (11:30 a.m., June 13, 2002).

7 *the inner consistency of reality:* J. R. R. Tolkien, "On Fairy Stories," in *Tales from the Perilous Realm* (New York: Houghton Mifflin, 2008), 362.

9 *what he thought . . . about anything:* Owen Barfield, *Owen Barfield on C. S. Lewis,* 122.

9 *cannot be taken in at a glance . . . by very intricate paths:* C. S. Lewis, *The Discarded Image: An Introduction to Medieval and Renaissance Literature,* 194.

9 *arbitrary:* C. S. Lewis, "On Stories," in *Of Other Worlds: Essays and Stories,* 13.

9 *the curve of every wave and the flight of every insect:* C. S. Lewis, *Letters to Malcolm,* 56.

10 *at first looks planless, though all is planned:* Lewis, *Discarded Image*, 194.

11 *puzzles to solve or secret writing to decode:* Laurence Harwood, *C. S. Lewis, My Godfather: Letters, Photos and Recollections*, 98.

11 tous exo: C. S. Lewis, "Rejoinder to Dr. Pittenger," in *God in the Dock*, 181.

11 *in the frankest way as friends should . . . I have never known a man more open about his private life:* George Sayer, "Jack on Holiday," in James T. Como, ed., *Remembering C. S. Lewis: Recollections of Those Who Knew Him* (San Francisco: Ignatius, 2005), 339.

12 *Jack never ceased to be secretive:* George Sayer, *Jack: C. S. Lewis and His Times*, 238.

12 *"Hallo, yoicks, gone that way" . . . followed his directions:* Ibid., 209.

CHAPTER 2: THE BEAM OF LIGHT

15 *In Your light we see light:* Psalm 36:9, NKJV.

16 *"Meditation in a Toolshed":* This essay appears in C. S. Lewis, *God in the Dock: Essays on Theology and Ethics*, 212–215.

18 *"The Man Born Blind":* This story appears in C. S. Lewis, *The Dark Tower and Other Stories* (Orlando, FL: Harcourt, 1977), 99–103.

19 *an indispensable tool of thought:* C. S. Lewis, *Surprised by Joy*, 218.

20 *[Christ] is the all-pervasive principle . . . whereby the universe holds together:* C. S. Lewis, *Miracles*, 121.

21 *We may ignore . . . walks everywhere incognito:* C. S. Lewis, *Letters to Malcolm*, 75.

21 *The fact which is in one respect . . . the Supernatural has been forgotten:* Lewis, *Miracles*, 64–65.

22 *breathing a new atmosphere . . . learning a subject:* C. S. Lewis, *Reflections on the Psalms*, 114.

23 *"On Stories":* This essay appears in C. S. Lewis, *Of Other Worlds*, 3–21.

24 *emotionally and atmospherically* as well as *logically:* C. S. Lewis, Letter to Arthur C. Clarke, January 20, 1954, in *Collected Letters*, Vol. 3, 412.

24 *weather:* C. S. Lewis, "On Stories," in *Of Other Worlds*, 7.

24–25 *A child is always thinking . . . you would know better:* C. S. Lewis, "Hamlet: The Prince or the Poem?" in *Selected Literary Essays*, 104–105.

25 *As is proper in romance, the inner meaning is carefully hidden:* C. S. Lewis, Letter to Arthur Greeves, July 18, 1916, in *Collected Letters*, Vol. 1, 216.

CHAPTER 3: THE SEVEN HEAVENS

27 *"The Planets":* This poem appears in C. S. Lewis, *Poems*, 12–15.

28 *influenza:* See C. S. Lewis, *The Discarded Image*, 110.

28 *winter passed and guilt forgiven:* C. S. Lewis, "The Planets," in *Poems*, 14.

29 *just and gentle:* Lewis, "Planets," 14.

29 Planet Narnia: *Planet Narnia* was the subject of the BBC documentary *The Narnia Code*, which is now available on DVD. For more information, see www.narniacode.com.

31 *tingling with life:* See C. S. Lewis, *English Literature in the Sixteenth Century, Excluding Drama*, 4.

35 *Gods and goddesses could always be used in a Christian sense:* Ibid., 342.

35 *The gods are God incognito and everyone is in the secret:* Ibid., 342.

35 *I have made no serious effort . . . It was not true:* Lewis, *Discarded Image*, 216.

36 *the highest point that poetry had ever reached:* C. S. Lewis, "Shelley, Dryden, and Mr. Eliot," in *Selected Literary Essays*, 203.

37 *The "space" of modern astronomy . . . satisfying in its harmony:* Lewis, *Discarded Image*, 99.

38 *In our world a star . . . only what it is made of:* C. S. Lewis, *The Voyage of the "Dawn Treader,"* 209.

39 *Lewis refers to this verse in his book* Out of the Silent Planet*:* See C. S. Lewis, *Out of the Silent Planet*, 127.

40–41 *The spheres transmit . . . much more, on plants and minerals:* Lewis, *Discarded Image*, 103–104.

41 *the lucrative . . . astrologically grounded predictions:* Ibid., 103.

41 *since the Bible strictly forbids that practice:* See, for example, Deuteronomy 4:19; 2 Kings 17:16; 21:3; 23:5; Job 31:26ff.; Jeremiah 8:2; 19:13.

41–42 *The characters of the planets . . . have a permanent value as spiritual symbols:* C. S. Lewis, "The Alliterative Metre," in *Selected Literary Essays*, 24.

42 *I give you the stars and I give you myself:* C. S. Lewis, *The Magician's Nephew*, 128.

42 *sun and moon and stars and Aslan himself:* C. S. Lewis, *The Silver Chair*, 182.

42 *If Aslan were really coming . . . would be assembled in his honor:* C. S. Lewis, *The Last Battle*, 19–20.

42 *perpetual* Gloria*:* See C. S. Lewis, *That Hideous Strength*, 324.

CHAPTER 4: JUPITER'S KINGLY CROWN: THE LION, THE WITCH AND THE WARDROBE

46 *peculiar, heady attraction:* C. S. Lewis, *Surprised by Joy*, 35.

46 *You must not believe . . . how they wrote their books:* C. S. Lewis, "It All Began with a Picture . . ." in *Of Other Worlds*, 42.

46 *If art is concealed it succeeds:* Ovid, *The Art of Love*, II.313.

46 *An influence which cannot evade our consciousness will not go very deep:* C. S. Lewis, "The Literary Impact of the Authorised Version," in *Selected Literary Essays*, 142.

46 *powerfully evoking secret associations:* C. S. Lewis, *Studies in Words*, 317.

46 *what the reader is made to do for himself has a particular importance in literature:* C. S. Lewis, "Imagery in the Last Eleven Cantos of Dante's 'Comedy,'" in *Studies in Medieval and Renaissance Literature*, 81.

46 *It all began with a picture:* See the essay with this title in C. S. Lewis, *Of Other Worlds*, 42.

47 *began with a picture of a Faun carrying an umbrella and parcels in a snowy wood:* Ibid., 42.

47 *there wasn't even anything Christian:* C. S. Lewis, "Sometimes Fairy Stories May Say Best What's to Be Said," in *Of Other Worlds*, 36.

47 *a queen on a sledge . . . a magnificent lion:* Ibid., 36.

47 *Aslan came bounding into it . . . pulled the whole story together:* Lewis, "It All Began," 42.

48 *lion-hearted . . . winter passed:* C. S. Lewis, "The Planets," in *Poems*, 14.

48 *winter overgone:* C. S. Lewis, *The Allegory of Love: A Study in Medieval Tradition*, 197.

48 *freezing wastes . . . unendurable cold:* C. S. Lewis, *That Hideous Strength*, 323.

48 *a melancholy voice:* C. S. Lewis, *The Lion, the Witch and the Wardrobe*, 12.

49 *always winter and never Christmas:* Ibid., 19.

49 *jollification:* Ibid., 16.

49 *When he bares his teeth . . . we shall have spring again:* Ibid., 79.

49 *he's the King:* Ibid., 78.

50 *is the King of the wood . . . is the King of Beasts?:* Ibid., 79.

50 *the true king . . . crown . . . standard . . . royal, solemn:* Ibid., 126.

50 *royal and strong:* Ibid., 129

50 *great, royal head:* Ibid., 149.

50 *is Kingly; but we must think of a King at peace, enthroned, taking his leisure, serene:* C. S. Lewis, *The Discarded Image,* 106.

50 *You are to be the Prince and—later on—the King:* Lewis, *Lion,* 39.

50 *to be a Prince (and later a King):* Ibid., 89.

50 *about Turkish Delight and about being a King:* Ibid., 70.

50 *when I'm King of Narnia . . . make some decent roads . . . thinking about being a King:* Ibid., 91.

50 *it didn't look now as if the Witch intended to make him a King:* Ibid., 114.

50 *Long live the true King!:* Ibid., 109.

50 *the castle where you are to be King . . . High King over all the rest:* Ibid., 129–130.

51 *Jupiter's red-pierced planet:* Charles Williams, "Taliessin in the Rose-Garden," in *Arthurian Poets: Charles Williams,* ed. David Llewellyn Dodds (Woodbridge, UK: The Boydell Press, 1991), 114–119.

51 *Jupiter, the planet of Kingship . . . the Divine King wounded on Calvary:* C. S. Lewis, *Arthurian Torso,* 2nd edition (Oxford: Oxford University Press, 1952), 150.

51 *Once a king or queen in Narnia, always a king or queen:* Lewis, *Lion,* 182.

52 *In the Great Hall of Cair Paravel . . . gold flashed and wine flowed:* Ibid., 182.

52–53 *cheerful and festive . . . It is obvious under which planet I was born:* Roger Lancelyn Green and Walter Hooper, *C. S. Lewis: A Biography,* 146.

53 *A supreme workman . . . unimaginative critics mistake for its laws:* C. S. Lewis, *Miracles,* 153.

53 *grasped the real and inward significance . . . a mere botch or failure of unity:* Ibid.

53 *bright as hollyberries:* Lewis, *Lion*, 106.
54 *Who does not need to be reminded of Jove?:* C. S. Lewis, "The Alliterative Metre," in *Selected Literary Essays*, 24.
55 *royal robes:* Lewis, *Lion, Witch, Wardrobe*, 56.
55 *you couldn't have found a robin with a redder chest:* Ibid., 60.
55 *apparent* minutiae: C. S. Lewis, "A Note on 'Comus,'" in *Studies in Medieval and Renaissance Literature*, 181.
56 *like a great star resting on the seashore:* Lewis, *Lion*, 130.

CHAPTER 5: THE WOODEN SHIELD OF MARS: PRINCE CASPIAN

57 *Above all, take the shield of faith:* Ephesians 6:16, KJV.
57 *brutal and ferocious:* C. S. Lewis, Letter to Sister Penelope CSMV, January 31, 1946, in *Collected Letters*, Vol. 2, 702.
58 *emotionally and atmospherically* as well as *logically:* C. S. Lewis, Letter to Arthur C. Clarke, January 20, 1954, in *Collected Letters*, Vol. 3, 412.
58 *the* click-click *of steel points in wooden shields:* C. S. Lewis, *That Hideous Strength*, 323.
59 *in the middle of a war:* C. S. Lewis, *Prince Caspian*, 103.
59 *the great War of Deliverance:* C. S. Lewis, *The Last Battle*, 205.
59 *to drive Miraz out of Narnia:* Lewis, *Caspian*, 78.
59 *I and my sons are ready . . . been thinking of a war . . . halls of high heaven:* Ibid., 78–79.
59 *Tarva, the Lord of Victory . . . Alambil, the Lady of Peace:* Ibid., 50.
59 *I know by the course of the planettes that there is a Knyght comynge:* Quoted in C. S. Lewis, *English Literature in the Sixteenth Century, Excluding Drama*, 151.
59 *is fortunate and means some great good for the sad realm of Narnia:* Lewis, *Caspian*, 50.
59 *quite possible that they might win a war and quite certain that they must wage one:* Ibid., 79.
60 *monomachy:* Ibid., 177.
60 *prunes and prism . . . Mrs. General:* See Charles Dickens's *Little Dorrit*, especially book 2, chapters 2 and 7.
60 *martial mouse . . . martial policy:* Lewis, *Caspian*, 79, 183.
60 *magic in the air:* Ibid., 27.
60 *the air of Narnia . . . all his old battles . . . back to him:* Ibid., 105.
60 *to harden . . . under the stars:* Ibid., 84.

60 *hard virtue of Mars:* C. S. Lewis, "The Adam at Night," in *Poems*, 45.

61 *knights-errant:* Lewis, *Caspian*, 11.

61 *rich suits of armor, like knights guarding the treasures:* Ibid., 25.

61 *Knight of the Noble Order of the Table . . . very dangerous knight:* Ibid., 177, 188.

61 *the character and influence of the planets are worked into the* Knight's Tale: C. S. Lewis, *The Discarded Image*, 198.

61 *Oh, bother, bother, bother. . . . Comes of being a Knight* and *a High King:* Lewis, *Caspian*, 194.

61–62 *morality up to the highest self-sacrifice . . . smallest gracefulness in etiquette:* C. S. Lewis, *Studies in Words*, 115.

62 *On the march . . . I'd as soon march as stand here talking . . . half a day's march . . . Count of the Western March:* Lewis, *Caspian*, 148, 149, 110, 177.

62 *Greenroof:* Ibid., 178.

63 *in a woody place . . . I can't see a yard in all these trees . . . thick and tangled . . . stoop under branches . . . through great masses of stuff like rhododendrons:* Ibid., 5, 7, 11.

63 *who cut down trees . . . could not be expected to know this:* Ibid., 64.

63 *wake the spirits of these trees . . . our enemies would go mad with fright:* Ibid., 80–81.

63–64 *Have you ever stood . . . The end of the world!:* Ibid., 196.

64 *divinely comfortable:* Ibid., 210.

65 *the inward significance of the whole work:* C. S. Lewis, *Miracles*, 153.

65 *the idea of the knight . . . the great Christian ideas:* C. S. Lewis, *Mere Christianity*, 119.

65 *by a supreme recovery of moral health and* martial *vigour . . . as in the olden times:* Winston Churchill, Speech to the House of Commons, October 5, 1938. See Roy Jenkins, *Churchill* (London: Macmillan, 2001), 528. Emphasis added.

65 *Peter's not using his shield properly . . . the full weight of his shoulder on my shield . . . and the rim of the shield drove into my wrist . . . the new bout went well . . . Peter now seemed to be able to make some use of his shield:* Lewis, *Caspian*, 191–193.

66 *knight of faith . . . not his sword but his shield:* C. S. Lewis, *Spenser's Images of Life*, 134.

66–67 *Aslan, who seemed larger than before . . . the trees stirred:* Lewis, *Caspian*, 156.

67 *Pale birch-girls were tossing their heads . . . in their various husky or creaking or wave-like voices:* Ibid., 157.

68 *Bother! . . . I've left my new torch in Narnia:* Ibid., 223.

CHAPTER 6: SUNLIGHT'S GOLDEN TREASURY: THE VOYAGE OF THE "DAWN TREADER"

69 *J. K. Rowling . . . rereads them now in adulthood whenever she finds a copy at hand:* See http://www.accio-quote.org/articles/2001/1001-sydney-renton.htm and http://www.accio-quote.org/articles/1998/0798-telegraph-bertodano.html.

70 *the uncomely common to cordial gold:* C. S. Lewis, "The Planets," in *Poems*, 13.

70 *many metals . . . alchemic beams:* C. S. Lewis, "Noon's Intensity," in *Poems*, 114.

70 *Break, Sun, my crusted earth . . . immortal metals . . . have their birth:* C. S. Lewis, "A Pageant Played in Vain," in *Poems*, 96.

70 *It lay face downward. . . . lit up from end to end:* C. S. Lewis, *The Voyage of the "Dawn Treader,"* 125.

71 *That water turns things into gold. . . . And that poor fellow on the bottom—well, you see:* Ibid., 126–127.

71 *It was heather that he dipped . . . The King who owned this island. . . . on pain of death, do you hear?:* Ibid., 127–128.

71–72 *swaggering, bullying idiots . . . Across the gray hillside above them . . . They knew it was Aslan:* Ibid., 128.

72 *This is a place with a curse on it:* Ibid., 129.

73 *the sun beat down:* Ibid., 83.

73 *the sun disappeared:* Ibid., 86.

73 *rent with bitter pangs . . . this way and that:* Homer, "Hymn to Apollo," lines 358–362, trans. Hugh G. Evelyn-White.

73 *began to feel as if he had fought and killed the dragon instead of merely seeing it die:* Lewis, *Voyage*, 86.

73 *with greedy, dragonish thoughts in his heart:* Ibid., 91.

73 *serpent with legs:* Ibid., 94.

73 *a monster cut off from the whole human race:* Ibid., 92.

74 *The very first tear he made was so deep that I thought it had gone right into my heart:* Ibid., 109.

74 *hurts and humbles:* Lewis, "Planets," 13.

74 *It hurt worse than anything I've ever felt . . . it hurts like billy-oh . . . and by the way, I'd like to apologize:* Lewis, *Voyage*, 109–110.

74 *Though they could not see the sunrise . . . the bay before them turned the color of roses:* Ibid., 111.

74 *makes men wise:* C. S. Lewis, *The Discarded Image*, 106.

74 *Don't fight! Push!:* Lewis, *Voyage*, 117.

74 *crimson dragons:* Ibid., 18.

75 *it was terrible—his eyes:* Ibid., 240.

76 *Up came the sun. . . . they were seeing beyond the End of the World into Aslan's country:* Ibid., 242–244.

76 *something so white . . . they could hardly look at it:* Ibid., 245.

76 *beheld only of eagle's eye:* Lewis, "Planets," 13.

76 *come and have breakfast . . . his snowy white flushed into tawny gold . . . scattering light from his mane:* Lewis, *Voyage*, 245–247.

77 *the very eastern end of the world . . . the utter East:* Ibid., 21.

77 *As Edmund said afterward . . . the beginning of the End of the World:* Ibid., 205.

77 *Every morning when the sun rose . . . but others disagreed:* Ibid., 130.

77 *there was no mistaking it:* Ibid., 205.

77 *The sun when it came up each morning looked twice, if not three times, its usual size:* Ibid., 218.

78 *tiny speck of light . . . a broad beam of light fell from it upon the ship . . . Lucy looked along the beam and presently saw something in it:* Ibid., 186–187.

78 *her fingers tingled when she touched it as if it were full of electricity:* Ibid., 151.

78 *shining mane . . . "I have been here all the time," said he, "but you have just made me visible":* Ibid., 158–159.

79 *become very commonplace and tiresome and it must have been the influence of those Pevensie children:* Ibid., 248.

79 *glitteringly alive . . . the older writers . . . is thoroughly dead:* C. S. Lewis, "De Audiendis Poetis," in *Studies in Medieval and Renaissance Literature*, 8.

CHAPTER 7: MIRROR OR MOONSHINE?: THE SILVER CHAIR

81 *The moon will shine like the sun . . . when the LORD binds up the bruises of his people:* Isaiah 30:26, NIV.

82 *behaving like a lunatic:* C. S. Lewis, *The Silver Chair*, 242.

82 *After that, the Head's friends . . . got her into Parliament where she lived happily ever after:* Ibid., 242.

83 *Every night there comes an hour . . . in my proper shape and sound mind:* Ibid., 156–157.

83 *Could Aslan have really meant them to unbind anyone—even a lunatic—who asked it in his name?:* Ibid., 167.

83 *damp little path:* Ibid., 4.

83 *grass [that] was soaking wet:* Ibid., 5.

83–84 *dripped off the laurel leaves . . . drip off the leaves . . . drops of water on the grass:* Ibid., 6, 8, 12.

84 *as you can in water (if you've learned to float really well) . . . wet fogginess . . . drenching her nearly to the waist . . . How wet I am!:* Ibid., 28, 30, 31, 32.

84 *watery:* Ibid., 34.

84 *muddy water . . . countless channels of water:* Ibid., 69, 66.

84 *watery . . . wet blanket:* Ibid., 234, 85, 105, 147.

84 *mist . . . damp bowstrings:* Ibid., 70, 77.

84–85 *countless streams . . . never short of water . . . full of rapids and waterfalls . . . sick of wind and rain . . . nasty wet business . . . too wet by now to bother about being a bit wetter . . . like cold water down the back . . . water for washing:* Ibid., 83, 84, 92, 96, 100, 154, 161.

85 *bright mornings . . . wet afternoons:* Ibid., 243.

85 *Lady Luna, in light canoe:* C. S. Lewis, "The Planets," in *Poems*, 12.

85 *silver ear-trumpet . . . silver mail . . . a silver chain:* Lewis, *Chair*, 41, 234, 43.

86 *Let me out, let me go back . . . very deep, the blue sky:* Ibid., 163–164.

86 *silver laughs:* Ibid., 178.

86 *What is this sun that you all speak of? Do you mean anything by the word? . . . You see that lamp . . . the whole Overworld and hangeth in the sky . . . Hangeth from what, my lord? . . . the sun is but a tale, a children's story:* Ibid., 178.

87 *is only sunlight at second hand:* C. S. Lewis, "Christianity and Culture," in *Christian Reflections*, 24.

87 *a stone that catches the sun's beam:* C. S. Lewis, "French Nocturne," in *The Collected Poems of C. S. Lewis*, 168.

87 *green as poison:* Lewis, *Chair*, 58.

87 *sick and green . . . the envious Moon:* William Shakespeare, *Romeo and Juliet*, II.ii.8, 4.

87 *dressed in black and altogether looked a little bit like Hamlet:* Lewis, *Chair*, 151.

87 *with his mind on the frontier of two worlds . . . unable quite to reject or quite to admit the supernatural:* C. S. Lewis, "Hamlet: The Prince or the Poem?" in *Selected Literary Essays*, 102.

87–88 *the freshness of the air . . . they must be on the top of a very high mountain . . . there was not a breath of wind:* Lewis, *Chair*, 13, 15.

88 *Here on the mountain . . . when you meet them there:* Ibid., 27.

88 *smothered . . . suffocating . . . sun and blue skies and wind and birds had not been only a dream . . . Many fall down, and few return to the sunlit lands:* Ibid., 143, 148, 140.

89 *Remember, remember, remember the signs. . . . let nothing turn your mind from following the signs:* Ibid., 27.

90 *fancies:* Ibid., 175.

90 *You can put nothing . . . which is the only world:* Ibid., 180.

90 *the bright skies of Overland . . . the great Lion . . . Aslan himself:* Ibid., 166.

90 *the sky and the sun and the stars . . . never was such a world:* Ibid., 174, 176.

90 *I've seen the sun coming up . . . couldn't look at him for brightness:* Ibid., 176–177.

90 *What is this* sun *that you all speak of? . . . There never was a* sun *. . . No. There never was a sun:* Ibid., 178–179.

90 *false, mocking fancy:* Lewis, "French Nocturne," 168.

90 *He knew it would hurt him badly enough; and so it did . . . the pain itself made Puddleglum's head . . . dissolving certain kinds of magic:* Lewis, *Chair*, 181.

91 *a great brightness of mid-summer sunshine:* Ibid., 237.

91 *blaze of sunshine . . . the light of a June day pours into a garage when you open the door:* Ibid., 12.

91 *a mirror filled with light:* C. S. Lewis, *Mere Christianity*, 149.

91 *a body ever more completely uncovered to the meridian blaze of the spiritual sun:* C. S. Lewis, *The Problem of Pain*, 156–157.

CHAPTER 8: MERCURY'S WINGED CAP: THE HORSE AND HIS BOY

94 *that shining suburb of the Sun:* C. S. Lewis, "The Birth of Language," in *Poems*, 10.

94 *Take some real mercury in a saucer . . . That is what "Mercurial" means:* C. S. Lewis, *The Discarded Image*, 108.

95 *Under the moonlight the sand . . . smooth water or a great silver tray:* C. S. Lewis, *The Horse and His Boy*, 128.

95   *Suddenly the sun rose . . . strewn with diamonds:* Ibid., 129.

95   *meeting selves, same but sundered:* C. S. Lewis, "The Planets," in *Poems,* 12.

95   *like two drops of quicksilver:* C. S. Lewis, *That Hideous Strength,* 275.

96   *twin-born progeny:* C. S. Lewis, "After Aristotle," in *Poems,* 80.

96   *horse-boy . . . a true horseman's seat:* Lewis, *Horse,* 54, 156.

96   *At least [Shasta] ran in the right direction . . . a child, a mere foal:* Ibid., 151.

96   *box . . . could ever equal Corin as a boxer . . . without a time-keeper for thirty-three rounds . . . Corin Thunder-Fist:* Ibid., 215, 224.

97   *neck to neck and knee to knee . . . side by side:* Ibid., 28–29.

97   *so used to quarrelling . . . go on doing it more conveniently:* Ibid., 224.

97   *everyone seemed to be going either to the left or right . . . either left or right . . . the road divided into two . . . if I stay at the crossroads I'm sure to be caught:* Ibid., 83, 105, 159.

98   *There's not a moment to lose:* Ibid., 127.

98   *not really been going as fast—not quite as fast—as he could:* Ibid., 142.

98   *swift horses:* Ibid., 41.

98   *swiftest of the galleys:* Ibid., 109.

98   *be swift:* Ibid., 119.

98   *far too swift:* Ibid., 139.

98   *swift of foot:* Ibid., 164.

98   *speed:* Ibid., 171.

98   *run now, without a moment's rest . . . run, run: always run:* Ibid., 145–146.

98   *a little heather running up before him . . . he had only to run:* Ibid., 153.

98   *with little wings on each side:* Ibid., 58.

98   Petasus*, or Mercurial hat:* C. S. Lewis, *Spenser's Images of Life,* 7.

99   *I had rather the feeling that . . . he wouldn't interfere:* Pauline Baynes, Letter to Walter Hooper, August 15, 1967, quoted in C. S. Lewis, *Collected Letters,* Vol. 2, 1020.

99   *lord of language:* Lewis, "Planets," 12.

99   *talking to one another very slowly about things that sounded dull:* Lewis, *Horse,* 4.

99 *loquacity . . . idle words:* Ibid., 9, 8.

99 *slaves' and fools' talk . . . Southern jargon:* Ibid., 14.

99 *Application to business . . . toward the rock of indigence:* Ibid., 4–5.

99 *As a costly jewel retains its value . . . the vile persons of our subjects:* Ibid., 111.

100 *Nothing is more suitable . . . than to endure minor inconveniences with constancy:* Ibid., 117.

100 *Easily in but not easily out, as the lobster said in the lobster pot!:* Ibid., 67.

100 *Maybe Apes will grow honest:* Ibid., 214.

100 *Come, live with me and you'll know me:* Ibid., 65.

100 *Nests before eggs:* Ibid., 73–74.

100 *for the only poetry they knew . . . a rocket seemed to go up inside their heads:* Ibid., 221.

100 *skyrockets of metaphor and allusion:* Lewis, *Hideous Strength*, 318.

100 *I wish you could talk, old fellow . . . dumb and witless like* their *horses:* Lewis, *Horse*, 11, 12.

101 *Don't you think it was bad luck to meet so many lions? . . . I was the lion . . . wakeful at midnight, to receive you:* Ibid., 164–165.

102 *merry multitude of meeting selves:* Lewis, "Planets," 12.

102 *"Who are you?" asked Shasta . . . it seemed to come from all round you as if the leaves rustled with it:* Lewis, *Horse*, 165.

103 *"Who are you?" he said . . . One who has waited long for you to speak:* Ibid., 163.

103 *gaped with open mouth and said nothing . . . after one glance at the Lion's face . . . he knew he needn't say anything:* Ibid., 164, 166.

103 *Strange to say, they felt no inclination to talk . . . there paced to and fro, each alone, thinking:* Ibid., 202.

103 *prayer without words is the best:* C. S. Lewis, *Letters to Malcolm*, 11.

103 *thou fair Silence:* C. S. Lewis, "The Apologist's Evening Prayer," in *Poems*, 129.

104 *a language more adequate:* C. S. Lewis, Letter to Arthur Greeves, October 18, 1931, in *Collected Letters*, Vol. 1, 977.

CHAPTER 9: APPLES ARE FROM VENUS: THE MAGICIAN'S NEPHEW

106 *love:* C. S. Lewis, *The Magician's Nephew*, 126.

106 *to and fro among the animals . . . one stag and one deer among all the deer:* Ibid., 124.

106 *bring up . . . children and grandchildren . . . children and grand-*
children shall be blessed . . . father and mother of many kings: Ibid.,
151, 152, 187.

106 *double-natured:* C. S. Lewis, *That Hideous Strength*, 320.

107 *The Lion opened his mouth. . . . "Narnia, Narnia, Narnia, awake.*
Love": Lewis, *Nephew*, 125–126.

108 *a warm, good smell of sun-baked earth and grass and flowers:* Ibid.,
162.

108 *grass growing, and grain bursting, / Flower unfolding:* C. S. Lewis,
"The Planets," in *Poems*, 13.

108 *all about crops being "safely gathered in":* Lewis, *Nephew*, 105.

108 *the valley grew green with grass. . . . The light wind could now be*
heard ruffling the grass: Ibid., 112.

108 *sprinkled with daisies and buttercups . . . primroses suddenly appear-*
ing in every direction . . . everything is bursting with life and growth:
Ibid., 114, 115, 120.

108 *you could almost feel the trees growing . . . very much alive . . . rich*
and warm . . . rich as plumcake: Ibid., 32, 47.

108 *can Venus arise in her beauty:* C. S. Lewis, *Spenser's Images of Life*,
129.

108 *rich reddish brown:* Lewis, *Nephew*, 41.

109 *there is even copper in the soil:* Lewis, *Hideous Strength*, 314.

109 *union with matter—the fertility of nature—is a continual conquest of*
death: Lewis, *Spenser's Images*, 56.

109 *Mother was ill and was going to—going to—die:* Lewis, *Nephew*, 6.

109 *while we ourselves can do nothing about mortality, Venus can:* Lewis,
Spenser's Images, 56.

110 *the fair Hesperian Tree . . . to save her blossoms, and defend her*
fruit / From the rash hand of bold incontinence: John Milton,
"Comus, a Mask," lines 393, 396–397, quoted in Lewis, *Spenser's*
Images, 24.

110 *real, natural, gentle sleep . . . sweet natural sleep:* Lewis, *Nephew*,
197, 176.

110 *breath's sweetness:* Lewis, "Planets," 12.

110 *laughter-loving:* See Homer's "Hymn to Aphrodite (V)."

110 *totally serious about Venus:* C. S. Lewis, *The Four Loves*, 99.

110–111 *All the other animals . . . laughed just as loud:* Lewis, *Nephew*, 129.

111 *Roars of laughter:* Ibid., 100.

111 *Venus Infernal:* See C. S. Lewis, *The Pilgrim's Regress,* 176, and *The Screwtape Letters,* 108.

112 *that great city:* Lewis, *Nephew,* 65.

112 *more and more of her wonderful beauty . . . A dem fine woman, sir, a dem fine woman. A superb creature . . . the Witch would fall in love with him . . . dem fine woman:* Ibid., 83, 202.

113 *beautiful . . . beyond comparison . . . so beautiful he could hardly bear it:* Ibid., 146, 106.

113 *such a sweetness . . . even alive and awake, before:* Ibid., 194.

113 *my sweet country of Narnia:* Ibid., 153.

113 *all the world derives the glorious features of beautie . . . all the world by thee at first was made:* Quoted in Lewis, *Spenser's Images,* 49, 43.

113 *With an unspeakable thrill, . . . when you looked round you, you saw them:* Lewis, *Nephew,* 115–116.

113 *is the reality behind . . . Venus; no woman ever conceived a child, no mare a foal, without Him:* C. S. Lewis, *Miracles,* 225.

113 *the planet of love:* C. S. Lewis, *Perelandra,* 32.

114 *Digory never spoke on the way back . . . shining tears in Aslan's eyes he became sure:* Lewis, *Nephew,* 178–179.

114 *but not to your joy or hers . . . better to die in that illness:* Ibid., 191.

114 *that there might be things more terrible even than losing someone you love by death:* Ibid., 191.

115 *Go. Pluck her an apple from the Tree:* Ibid., 191.

115 *She has unwearying strength and endless days. . . . they do not always like it:* Ibid., 190.

115 *Ask for the Morning Star and take (thrown in) / Your earthly love:* C. S. Lewis, "Five Sonnets," in *Poems,* 126–127.

CHAPTER 10: SATURN'S SANDS OF TIME: THE LAST BATTLE

117 *was once Saturn:* C. S. Lewis, *English Literature in the Sixteenth Century, Excluding Drama,* 356.

118 *Our traditional picture of Father Time with the scythe is derived from earlier pictures of Saturn:* C. S. Lewis, *The Discarded Image,* 105.

118 *that his name was Father Time, and that he would wake on the day the world ended:* C. S. Lewis, *The Last Battle,* 171.

118 *That is the god Saturn. . . . the end of the world:* For a facsimile of this typescript of *The Silver Chair,* see the illustrations between pages 126 and 127 of my *Planet Narnia.*

118 *the last planet old and ugly:* C. S. Lewis, "The Planets," in *Poems*, 15.

119 *In the last days of Narnia:* Lewis, *Battle*, 3.

119 *About three weeks later the* last *of the Kings of Narnia:* Ibid., 16, emphasis added.

119 *last friends . . . And then the last battle of the last King of Narnia began:* Ibid., 147.

119 *He was so old . . . ugliest, most wrinkled Ape you can imagine:* Ibid., 3.

119 *ten times uglier:* Ibid., 32.

119 *I'm so very old . . . because I'm so old that I'm so wise:* Ibid., 35.

119 *mountain of centuries . . . more and still more time:* C. S. Lewis, *That Hideous Strength*, 323.

119 *daunted with darkness:* Lewis, "Planets," 14–15.

119 *disastrous events:* Lewis, *Discarded Image*, 105.

119 *dreary and disastrous dawn:* Lewis, *Battle*, 179.

120 *shall probably die . . . almost tired to death:* Ibid., 6, 8.

120 *If we had died before today we should have been happy:* Ibid., 25.

120 *Would it not be better to be dead than to have this horrible fear?:* Ibid., 30.

120 *It would have been better if we'd died before all this began:* Ibid., 45.

120 *to die in the salt-pits of Pugrahan:* Ibid., 78.

120 *filled with dead Narnians:* Ibid., 103.

120 *more like a mouth:* Ibid., 146.

121 *discourtesy:* Ibid., 182.

121 *hundreds and thousands of years . . . till you could hardly remember their names:* Ibid., 99.

121 *And as he went on . . . till it got thin and misty from distance:* Ibid., 100.

121 *On the contrary, it is just when there seems to be most of Heaven already here that I come nearest to longing for the* patria . . . *is the bright frontispiece:* C. S. Lewis, Letter to Dom Bede Griffiths, November 5, 1954, in *Collected Letters*, Vol. 3, 522–523.

122 *had only been the cover and the title page . . . they were beginning Chapter One . . . every chapter is better than the one before:* Lewis, *Battle*, 210–211.

122 *horrible thoughts went through his mind . . . remembered the nonsense . . . knew that the whole thing must be a cheat:* Ibid., 47.

123 *And he called out, "Aslan! Aslan! Aslan!* . . . *And he felt somehow stronger:* Ibid., 49–50.

123 *may be for us the door to Aslan's country and we shall sup at his table tonight:* Ibid., 146.

123 *In the name of Aslan let us go forward* . . . *I serve the real Aslan* . . . *the adventure that Aslan would send* . . . *we are all between the paws of the true Aslan* . . . *Aslan to our aid!* . . . *Well done, last of the Kings of Narnia who stood firm at the darkest hour:* Ibid., 68, 82, 106, 121, 134, 167.

124 *seventh son* . . . *seventh in descent:* Ibid., 185, 57.

124 *disastrous conjunctions of the planets* . . . *the stars never lie:* Ibid., 19.

124 *is not the slave of the stars but their Maker:* Ibid., 20.

124 *Heaven's hermitage:* Lewis, "Planets," 15.

125 *overmatched:* Lewis, *Hideous Strength*, 323.

125 *"The Turn of the Tide":* See C. S. Lewis, *Poems*, 49–51.

125 *unstiffened* . . . *bitingly cold* . . . *delicious foamy coolness* . . . *the summer sea* . . . *was that of a day in early summer:* Lewis, *Battle*, 158, 199, 150, 156.

125 *"Isn't it wonderful?" said Lucy.* . . . *Eustace after he had tried:* Ibid., 199.

126 *Saturnocentric:* C. S. Lewis, "Donne and Love Poetry," in *Selected Literary Essays*, 113.

126 *"Further in and higher up!"* . . . *somehow set them tingling all over:* Lewis, *Battle*, 176.

126 *the gathering of the Church Triumphant in Heaven* . . . *the fruit of Time, or of the Spheres:* C. S. Lewis, "Imagery in the Last Eleven Cantos of Dante's 'Comedy,'" in *Studies in Medieval and Renaissance Literature*, 91.

CHAPTER 11: THE CANDLESTICK

129 *I saw a gold menorah with seven branches, and in the center, the Son of Man:* Revelation 1:12-13, The Message.

129 *about Christ:* C. S. Lewis, Letter to Anne Jenkins, March 5, 1961, in *Collected Letters*, Vol. 3, 1244.

129–130 *[Christ] is the all-pervasive principle* . . . *whereby the universe holds together:* C. S. Lewis, *Miracles*, 121.

130 *jollification:* C. S. Lewis, *The Lion, the Witch and the Wardrobe*, 16.

130 *spiritual symbols* . . . *permanent value:* C. S. Lewis, "The Alliterative Metre," in *Selected Literary Essays*, 24.

131 *at the back of all the stories:* C. S. Lewis, *The Horse and His Boy,* 208.

132 *Of Saturn we know more than enough . . . but who does not need to be reminded of Jove?:* Lewis, "Alliterative Metre," 24.

132 *an idea . . . tried it out to the full:* Charles Wrong, "A Chance Meeting," in James T. Como, ed., *Remembering C. S. Lewis: Recollections of Those Who Knew Him* (San Francisco: Ignatius, 2005), 212.

132 *a model or symbol, certain to fail us in the long run and, even while we use it, requiring correction from other models:* C. S. Lewis, *The Four Loves,* 126.

133 *My idea of God is not a divine idea:* C. S. Lewis, *A Grief Observed,* 66.

134 *I hope no one will think . . . respecting each and idolising none:* C. S. Lewis, *The Discarded Image,* 222.

135 *paradoxes, fancies, anecdotes . . . well worth taking seriously:* C. S. Lewis, *That Hideous Strength,* 318.

135 *But Edmund said they had only been pretending . . . very careful consideration:* Lewis, *Lion,* 47.

135–136 *"O-o-oh!" said Susan suddenly. . . . Why, I do believe we've got into Lucy's wood after all:* Ibid., 54–55.

136 *"In our world," said Eustace . . . but only what it is made of:* C. S. Lewis, *The Voyage of the "Dawn Treader,"* 209.

CHAPTER 12: THE TELESCOPE

139 *For now we see through a glass, darkly; but then face to face:* 1 Corinthians 13:12, KJV.

139 *Do you ever notice Venus . . . almost better than Jupiter:* C. S. Lewis, Letter to Laurence Harwood, December 31, 1946, in *Collected Letters,* Vol. 2, 751.

141 *When you come to knowing God . . . cannot be reflected in a dusty mirror as clearly as in a clean one:* C. S. Lewis, *Mere Christianity,* 164.

142 *While in other sciences . . . like the Moon seen through a dirty telescope:* Ibid., 164–165.

143 *The one really adequate instrument . . . everyone has forgotten all about him, but the real science is still going on:* Ibid., 165.

144 *If in some twilit hour . . . a harmless wraith and means nothing but good:* C. S. Lewis, Letter to the Master and Fellows of Magdalene College, October 25, 1963, in *Collected Letters,* Vol. 3, 1471.

145 *The perfect never say anything of themselves. . . . They only say what the Spirit suffers them to say:* Archimandrite Sophrony, *The Monk of Mount Athos,* trans. Rosemary Edmonds (Crestwood, NY: St. Vladimir's Seminary Press, 1973), 40.

145 *winter passed / And guilt forgiven:* C. S. Lewis, "The Planets," in *Poems,* 14.

FOR FURTHER READING

WORKS BY C. S. LEWIS

The Allegory of Love: A Study in Medieval Tradition (Oxford: Oxford University Press, 1958 [1936]).

Christian Reflections, ed. Walter Hooper (Grand Rapids, MI: Eerdmans, 1995 [1967]).

Collected Letters, Volume 1, ed. Walter Hooper (New York: HarperCollins, 2000).

Collected Letters, Volume 2, ed. Walter Hooper (New York: HarperCollins, 2004).

Collected Letters, Volume 3, ed. Walter Hooper (New York: HarperCollins, 2006).

The Collected Poems of C. S. Lewis, ed. Walter Hooper (London: HarperCollins, 1994).

The Discarded Image: An Introduction to Medieval and Renaissance Literature (Cambridge: Cambridge University Press, 1964).

English Literature in the Sixteenth Century, Excluding Drama (Oxford: Clarendon Press, 1954).

An Experiment in Criticism (Cambridge: Cambridge University Press, 1961).

The Four Loves (Orlando, FL: Harcourt, 1988 [1960]).

God in the Dock: Essays on Theology and Ethics, ed. Walter Hooper (Grand Rapids, MI: Eerdmans, 1970).

A Grief Observed (New York: HarperCollins, 1996 [1961]).

The Horse and His Boy (New York: HarperTrophy, 1982 [1954]).

The Last Battle (New York: HarperTrophy, 1984 [1956]).

Letters to Malcolm: Chiefly on Prayer (Orlando, FL: Harcourt, 1992 [1964]).

The Lion, the Witch and the Wardrobe (New York: HarperTrophy, 1978 [1950]).

The Magician's Nephew (New York: HarperTrophy, 1983 [1955]).

Mere Christianity (New York: HarperCollins, 1980 [1952]).

Miracles: A Preliminary Study, 2nd edition (New York: HarperCollins, 1974 [1960]).

Of Other Worlds: Essays and Stories, ed. Walter Hooper (Orlando, FL: Harcourt, 1994 [1966]).

Out of the Silent Planet (New York: Scribner, 1996 [1938]).

Perelandra (New York: Scribner, 1972 [1943]).

The Pilgrim's Regress, 3rd edition (Grand Rapids, MI: Eerdmans, 1992 [1943]).

Poems, ed. Walter Hooper (Orlando, FL: Harcourt, 2002 [1964]).

A Preface to Paradise Lost (Oxford: Oxford University Press, 1984 [1942]).

Prince Caspian (New York: HarperTrophy, 1979 [1951]).

The Problem of Pain (New York: HarperCollins, 1996 [1940]).

Reflections on the Psalms (Orlando, FL: Harcourt, 1986 [1958]).

The Screwtape Letters (New York: HarperCollins, 1996 [1942]).

Selected Literary Essays, ed. Walter Hooper (Cambridge: Cambridge University Press, 1967).

The Silver Chair (New York: HarperTrophy, 1981 [1953]).

Spenser's Images of Life, ed. Alastair Fowler (Cambridge: Cambridge University Press, 1967).

Studies in Medieval and Renaissance Literature (Cambridge: Cambridge University Press, 1966).

Studies in Words (Cambridge: Cambridge University Press, 1967 [1960]).

Surprised by Joy (Orlando, FL: Harcourt, 1955).

That Hideous Strength (New York: Scribner, 1974 [1945]).

Till We Have Faces (Orlando, FL: Harcourt, 1984 [1956]).

The Voyage of the "Dawn Treader" (New York: HarperTrophy, 1980 [1952]).

WORKS ABOUT C. S. LEWIS AND NARNIA

Barfield, Owen, *Owen Barfield on C. S. Lewis*, ed. G. B. Tennyson (Middletown, CT: Wesleyan University Press, 1989).

Carpenter, Humphrey, *The Inklings: C. S. Lewis, J. R. R. Tolkien, Charles Williams, and Their Friends* (New York: HarperCollins, 2006).

Christensen, Michael J., *C. S. Lewis on Scripture: His Thoughts on the Nature of Biblical Inspiration, the Role of Revelation, and the Question of Inerrancy* (Nashville: Abingdon, 1989).

Downing, David C., *Planets in Peril: A Critical Study of C. S. Lewis's Ransom Trilogy* (Amherst, MA: University of Massachusetts Press, 1992).

Edwards, Bruce L., ed., *The Taste of the Pineapple: Essays on C. S. Lewis as Reader, Critic and Imaginative Writer* (Bowling Green, OH: Bowling Green State University Popular Press, 1988).

Glyer, Diana Pavlac, *The Company They Keep: C. S. Lewis and J. R. R. Tolkien as Writers in Community* (Kent, OH: The Kent State University Press, 2007).

Green, Roger Lancelyn and Walter Hooper, *C. S. Lewis: A Biography*, revised edition (Orlando, FL: Harcourt, 1994).

Harwood, Laurence, *C. S. Lewis, My Godfather: Letters, Photos and Recollections* (Downers Grove, IL: InterVarsity, 2007).

Holmer, Paul, *C. S. Lewis: The Shape of His Faith and Thought* (New York: Harper & Row, 1976).

Hooper, Walter, *C. S. Lewis: A Complete Guide to His Life and Works* (San Francisco: HarperCollins, 1996).

Jacobs, Alan, *The Narnian: The Life and Imagination of C. S. Lewis* (New York: HarperCollins, 2005).

MacSwain, Robert and Michael Ward, eds., *The Cambridge Companion to C. S. Lewis* (Cambridge: Cambridge University Press, 2010).

Manlove, C. N., *The Chronicles of Narnia: The Patterning of a Fantastic World* (New York: Twayne, 1993).

Martin, Thomas L., ed., *Reading the Classics with C. S. Lewis* (Grand Rapids, MI: Baker Academic, 2000).

Martindale, Wayne, *Beyond the Shadowlands: C. S. Lewis on Heaven and Hell* (Wheaton, IL: Crossway Books, 2005).

Menuge, Angus J. L., ed., *C. S. Lewis: Lightbearer in the Shadowlands: The Evangelistic Vision of C. S. Lewis* (Wheaton, IL: Crossway Books, 1997).

Miller, Laura. *The Magician's Book: A Skeptic's Adventures in Narnia* (New York: Little, Brown, 2008).

Mills, David, ed., *The Pilgrim's Guide: C. S. Lewis and the Art of Witness* (Grand Rapids, MI: Eerdmans, 1998).

Myers, Doris T., *C. S. Lewis in Context* (Kent, OH: The Kent State University Press, 1991).

Payne, Leanne, *Real Presence: The Christian Worldview of C. S. Lewis as Incarnational Reality* (Grand Rapids, MI: Baker Books, 2002).

Sayer, George, *Jack: C. S. Lewis and His Times* (San Francisco: Harper & Row, 1988).

Schakel, Peter J., *Reading with the Heart: The Way into Narnia* (Grand Rapids, MI: Eerdmans, 1979).

Schakel, Peter J. and Charles A. Huttar, eds., *Word and Story in C. S. Lewis* (Columbia, MO: University of Missouri Press, 1991).

Ward, Michael, *Planet Narnia: The Seven Heavens in the Imagination of C. S. Lewis* (New York: Oxford University Press, 2008).

Watson, George, ed., *Critical Essays on C. S. Lewis* (Aldershot, UK: Scolar Press, 1992).

WORKS ABOUT THE PLANETS AND THE PRE-COPERNICAN HEAVENS

Cantor, Norman F., *Inventing the Middle Ages: The Lives, Works, and Ideas of the Great Medievalists of the Twentieth Century* (Cambridge: Lutterworth Press, 1991).

Chapman, Allan, *Gods in the Sky: Astronomy, Religion, and Culture from the Ancients to the Renaissance* (London: Channel 4 Books, 2002).

Danielson, Dennis Richard, ed., *The Book of the Cosmos: Imagining the Universe from Heraclitus to Hawking* (Cambridge, MA: Perseus Publishing, 2000).

Dante Alighieri, *The Divine Comedy, Vol. III: Paradise*, trans. Dorothy L. Sayers and Barbara Reynolds (London: Penguin, 1962).

Eade, J. C., *The Forgotten Sky: A Guide to Astrology in English Literature* (Oxford: Clarendon Press, 1984).

Freeland, Guy and Anthony Corones, *1543 and All That: Image and Word, Change and Continuity in the Proto-Scientific Revolution* (Dordrecht: Kluwer Academic Publishers, 2000).

Funkenstein, Amos, *Theology and the Scientific Imagination: From the Middle Ages to the Seventeenth Century* (Princeton: Princeton University Press, 1986).

Harrison, H. M., *Voyager in Space and Time: The Life of John Couch Adams, Cambridge Astronomer* (Lewes: Book Guild, 1994).

Jaki, Stanley L., *God and the Cosmologists* (Edinburgh: Scottish Academic Press, 1989).

Kay, Richard, *Dante's Christian Astrology* (Philadelphia: University of Pennsylvania Press, 1994).

Kuhn, Thomas S., *The Structure of Scientific Revolutions* (Chicago: Chicago University Press, 1962).

Seznec, Jean, *The Survival of the Pagan Gods: The Mythological Tradition and Its Place in Renaissance Humanism and Art*, trans. Barbara F. Sessions (New York: Pantheon, 1953).

Sorbel, Dava, *The Planets* (London: Fourth Estate, 2005).

Zerubavel, Eviatar, *The Seven Day Circle: The History and Meaning of the Week* (New York: Macmillan, 1985).

SCRIPTURE INDEX

DISCUSSION GUIDE

CHAPTER 1: THE MYSTERY

1. How important were the stories you read as a child in making you the person you are now?

2. In his teaching, Jesus often told parables that weren't immediately easy to understand. What are the benefits of teaching by means of stories?

3. As well as being open and candid, C. S. Lewis could sometimes be secretive, private, and even deliberately misleading (as with the fox-hunters). Is it ever right not to tell the whole truth?

4. Before being introduced to this book, had you ever wondered whether the Chronicles of Narnia might contain a hidden level of meaning? Explain. What do you think are the merits of exploring this idea?

CHAPTER 2: THE BEAM OF LIGHT

1. Good ideas often come when you're relaxed and idling in one of the three B's: the bed, the bus, or the bath. Do you think idling can be a good thing at times? Explain.

2. Which do you generally prefer: looking *at* the beam of light or looking *along* the beam of light? Is there a situation where you might prefer the other? Explain.

3. Lewis believed that coming to know God is more like "breathing a new atmosphere" than it is like "learning a subject." Do you agree with Lewis? Why or why not?

CHAPTER 3: THE SEVEN HEAVENS

1. In English, the days of the week are named after the seven planets and their associated "gods." Does knowing this make any difference to you, either for good or for bad?

2. When you look out at the night sky, which word immediately comes to mind: *space* or *heavens*? Does it make any difference?

3. In *The Voyage of the "Dawn Treader,"* Eustace says that a star is "a huge ball of flaming gas" and Ramandu tells him that "that is not what a star is, but only what it is made of." How much do you agree with this?

CHAPTER 4: JUPITER'S KINGLY CROWN

1. In *The Lion, the Witch and the Wardrobe*, the children become kings and queens at the end of the story, and in the Bible we are told that God will "give a crown of life to those who love Him" (James 1:12). What are the advantages of thinking about the Christian life in royal terms? What are the disadvantages?

2. Lewis nearly always uses winter to symbolize things that are bad or undesirable and summer to symbolize things that are good and lovely. Do you think of winter and summer in this way? Explain.

3. Do you think Lewis was wise to include Father Christmas in *The Lion, the Witch and the Wardrobe*? Why or why not?

CHAPTER 5: THE WOODEN SHIELD OF MARS

1. In *Prince Caspian* the trees adore Aslan, and in the Bible we are told that "the trees of the field clap their hands for joy" (Isaiah 55:12). How is it possible for the nonhuman parts of creation to worship God?

2. Why did Lewis value the knightly ideal so much, and how helpful do you find it to think about the Christian life in martial terms?

3. Reepicheep is described as a "martial mouse." Why do you think Lewis made the most martial Narnian character a mouse?

CHAPTER 6: SUNLIGHT'S GOLDEN TREASURY

1. In *The Voyage of the "Dawn Treader,"* Eustace is greedy for gold while Caspian is greedy for Aslan's country. Is one kind of dragonish greed worse than the other? Why or why not?

2. Lucy makes Aslan visible though he has been present with her "all the time," and in the Bible Jesus says, "I am the light of the world" (John 8:12). Is light something we see or something we see by? Explain.

3. What sort of influence, if any, does the Sun have on your mood? How helpful do you find Solar imagery as a way of talking about the Christian life?

CHAPTER 7: MIRROR OR MOONSHINE?

1. In *The Silver Chair*, Aslan says to Jill, "Remember, remember, remember the signs." What place does learning by habit have in the Christian life?

2. After Puddleglum stamps on the fire, Lewis writes, "There is nothing like a good shock of pain for dissolving certain kinds of magic." Have you seen this principle at work in your own life or in the world at large? Explain.

3. Lewis reminds us that moonlight is sunlight at second hand and that the word *moonshine* means "nonsense, foolishness." How is the Moon's imagery used to portray foolishness in *The Silver Chair*? Does it provide any useful cautions for your own life?

CHAPTER 8: MERCURY'S WINGED CAP

1. In *The Horse and His Boy*, when Shasta first sees Aslan's face, he doesn't say anything but falls at his feet. What part does silence play in the Christian life?

2. Aslan says "there was only one lion" but speaks his name, "Myself," in three different voices. How much do you think of God as one and how much do you think of Him as three— Father, Son, and Holy Spirit? What does it matter?

3. In *The Horse and His Boy*, Shasta and Aravis come to love Narnian poetry and a Narnian lord wears a winged cap (suggesting thoughts that can take flight and bring freedom). What value do you attach to poetry and the life of the mind?

CHAPTER 9: APPLES ARE FROM VENUS

1. In *The Magician's Nephew*, both Aslan and Jadis are described as beautiful. How can the evil Jadis be beautiful? What role should beauty play in the Christian life?

2. Aslan says to the Narnians, "Laugh and fear not." When you think of Christianity, do you think of laughter? Why or why not?

3. Digory has to find a magic apple and give it to Aslan rather than using it, as the Witch suggests, to heal his own mother. This makes Digory sad, but why is it the loving thing to do?

CHAPTER 10: SATURN'S SANDS OF TIME

1. In *The Last Battle*, Tirian calls out to Aslan for help and "there was no change in the night or the wood, but there began to be a kind of change inside Tirian." How is it that Tirian changes even though the night and the wood do not change?

2. Tirian says it would be a "discourtesy" if he didn't weep for the death of Narnia, and in the Bible Jesus says, "Blessed are those who mourn" (Matthew 5:4). Why is it good sometimes to cry and lament?

3. What did Lewis mean by the word *Saturnocentric*, and why did he think that Saturn was not the center of the seven planetary "spiritual symbols"? Which planet did Lewis consider to be symbolically central? What is the significance of that?

CHAPTER 11: THE CANDLESTICK

1. Lewis said that the Narnia series was "about Christ." In each Chronicle, Lewis uses the planetary symbolism to structure the whole story: not just the plot, but also the portrayal of Aslan and all sorts of ornamental details too. What does this tell us of Lewis's beliefs about Christ?

2. What are the benefits of having seven different symbols of Christ? What are the drawbacks?

3. There are various questions we can ask about the universe such as "Why is it there?" "Who made it?" "How was it made?" "What is it made of?" Which sorts of questions did Lewis think were most important? Which sorts of questions do you think are most important?

CHAPTER 12: THE TELESCOPE

1. How did John Couch Adams discover Neptune, and why did Lewis think this discovery was so interesting?

2. Lewis pictured each Christian person as a "telescope" trained on God, so why did he think "the Christian community" so vital to the Christian life?

3. The psalmist wrote that "the heavens are telling the glory of God" (Psalm 19:1) and the apostle Paul said that the heavens spoke "the word of Christ" (Romans 10:18). Do you agree that the seven heavens are the Christian symbolic code that Lewis used to structure the Narnia Chronicles? Why or why not?

4. Before reading *The Narnia Code*, did you know about Lewis's academic interests in pre-Copernican cosmology? If not, how has reading about Lewis's love of the medieval planets enriched your understanding of his work?